YAKUZA TATTOO

入れ墨

YAKUZA TATTOO

入れ墨

Andreas Johansson

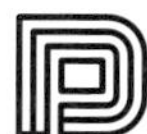

Yakuza Tattoo

Andreas Johansson

© 2019 Dokument Press & Andreas Johansson
Paperback edition, second printing
Printed in Poland 2022
ISBN 978-91-88369-21-5

Text & Photo: Andreas Johansson
Editor: Björn Almqvist
Photo Editing: Svensk Bokproduktion
Graphic Design: Martin Ander

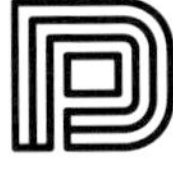

DOKUMENT PRESS

Dokument Press
Box 773
120 02 Årsta
Sweden
www.dokument.org

Beginnings

This book will give the reader a unique insight into the world of the yakuza, the Japanese mafia. The material deals with the symbols of the yakuza, and as the title might give away, it focuses on their tattoos. It primarily contains photographs, but also observations and excerpts from interviews with members of the yakuza.

Traditional Japanese tattoo designs are indeed rich in Japanese culture. They contain, for example, mythological figures like gods, and heroes. As a researcher of the history of religions, I am of course curious about the way non-religious groups use mythological symbols in their organizations. It was during the summer of 2014 that I first came into contact with Ken-San, a member of Masuda-gumi, which is connected to Yamaguchi-gumi, the largest yakuza organization in Japan. Since my area of research mainly focuses on the use of symbols, I told Ken-San that I was interested in photographing the yakuzas' tattoos. He gave me permission to do so, and I started to interview him about what his body art means to him. I believe that my interest in symbols and not the organization per se, plus the fact that I am a researcher and not a journalist, are the two main reasons why I was able to gain access to this otherwise closed world.

Tattoos can get you killed in Japan. At least that is the fate that met one young member of a yakuza family when he was spotted in another gang's territory, exposing his tattoos. An argument ensued, and later he was killed. Yakuza bear their tattoos with pride, but they also cover them up in certain situations. On one occasion we were having dinner in a nice restaurant. One of the members kept his jacket on. When I asked him why, he replied that he was only wearing a t-shirt underneath. If he took it off, he would expose his yakuza tattoos, and this would not be appreciated by the owner and the other customers. Why, then, do they tattoo themselves? Yakuza tattoos can win a member a great deal of respect in the Japanese underworld, and in prison they can serve as a means to ensure protection. The reason why tattoos are associated with criminals is that most yakuza have them, and tattoos also have historical connections to a criminal lifestyle. In Japanese society, traditional tattoos are better known as *irezumi*, which literally means insertion of ink. One of the first things that I learned from the yakuza was that they prefer the term *irezumi* over tattoo. *Irezumi* seems to have a deeper spiritual meaning.

In ancient Japan, tattoos were used as a way of punishing criminals. Between 400 and 700 CE, lawbreakers were marked with tattoos on their foreheads or black circles around their arms to signify the type of crime they had committed, where they were from, and how many times they had been convicted. This practice was eventually stopped since it was time-consuming and criminals got additional tattoos to cover up their criminal markings.

However, to make the generalization that criminals are the only people with *irezumi* in Japan is unfair and inaccurate. Archaeological findings of clay figures in graves suggest that tattoos had a religious significance. Chinese documents dated in 297 CE indicate that Japanese men had tattoos on their faces and bodies. There is also evidence that priests in the sixteenth century had tattoos of a religious nature, and it is also believed that some lovers got them in order to show their devotion to one another.

Japanese *irezumi* art, as we know it today, started to develop during the Edo period in the eighteenth century. As it became increasingly popular, state institutions introduced a ban on the practice. This ban gained considerable force in 1842, and the situation remained much the same until 1948. Some of the groups that had *irezumi* were firemen and laborers. One image that was particularly popular among firemen was the dragon due to its association with water.

The popularity of, for example, sumo wrestling and Kabuki theater led to an increasing demand for illustrations of wrestlers and actors to be used in advertising in publications. This resulted in the development of Japanese woodblock printing. These prints are known as "pictures of the floating world", or *ukiyoe*. They became very popular irrespective of social class. Two of the most famous artists from this period were Utamaro Kitagawa (1750–1806) and Kuniyoshi Utagawa (1797[8]–1861). However, the best known print from this period is probably Katsushika Hokusai's (1760–1849) *The Great Wave off Kanagwa*. These processes went hand in hand with the growth of *irezumi* culture and can even be traced to the present day. Many contemporary *irezumi* artists have an alias that begins with "Hori", which means to carve just like the masters of woodblock printing. Not only did the artists themselves create motifs for *irezumi*, their paintings also inspired *irezumi* artists in creating their own designs, a relationship that still lives on to this day.

At the close of the Edo period in 1868, Japan began to open up a bit more to the West. Somewhat paradoxically, the forbidden *irezumi* sparked a lot of interest among western visitors to Japan. It thus became legal for westerners to get Japanese *irezumi*, and this new fascination with *irezumi* artistry went both ways. Japanese *irezumi* masters started to use tattoo guns in combination with traditional *tebori* (usually applied using a bamboo rod with an iron needle at the end). Ideas of different styles of *irezumi* were shared, and the exchange of western and Japanese influences also brought new colors to Japan's old style of tattooing. One of the most notable American tattoo artists, Sailor Jerry, was influenced by Japanese *irezumi.* He subsequently brought the style back with him when he returned to the States after a trip to Japan.

You may wonder why a Swedish scholar of the history of religions is interested in yakuza tattoos and why he uses his camera to document them. The role of a historian of religions is not only to analyze and understand religious texts or institutions, but also, among other things, to seek knowledge about the ways non–religious institutions use religious language and symbols. What advantage, then, does the historian of religions have? In his book *Morgonrodnad: Socialismens stil och mytologi,* historian of religions Stefan Arvidsson states that, "[in] general, a historian of religions puts more emphasis on symbolism, the rhetorical form and the visual expression of a story and/or image" (Arvidsson 2016:15).

This is the one thing I have found to be lacking in the books I have read about the yakuza. Although earlier research mentions the different symbols of the yakuza, there is hardly any discussion on why they choose certain tattoos and what these symbolize. The focus has been on, for example, organizational structure and transnational connections.

Let's be honest, it may take months, even years of preparations before you can begin to study a culture that is different from your own. You may need to learn a new language as well as various features particular to that culture in order to get a deeper understanding of your chosen topic. For the purposes of this book, I have not spent years in Japan learning Japanese, and my access to the Japanese mafia was limited, which is hardly surprising. However, I still believe that this book will give you a unique insight into the symbolic universe of the yakuza. This is because it takes a visual approach to presenting empirical data as I mostly used my camera to document the symbols they use. Even though it has its limits, this method still provides an accurate visual presentation of these symbols. While the pictures in this book only constitute a selection of the material, the information is detailed.

Anthropologists John Collier and Malcolm Collier have argued in favor of using a camera in the field as it allows you to gain quicker access to your subjects. When you bring your camera into the "field", it implies that you have an "active job": "the observer is introduced as someone who has a job to do; he will be as active as they are" (Collier & Collier 1987:22). Collier and Collier use the word "can-opener" when they describe the benefits of using a camera in the field. It opens up possibilities for interacting with the people you photograph. They want to see the pictures, and they want to educate you about what you see.

This is exactly what happened to me when I used my camera in the field. It offered me

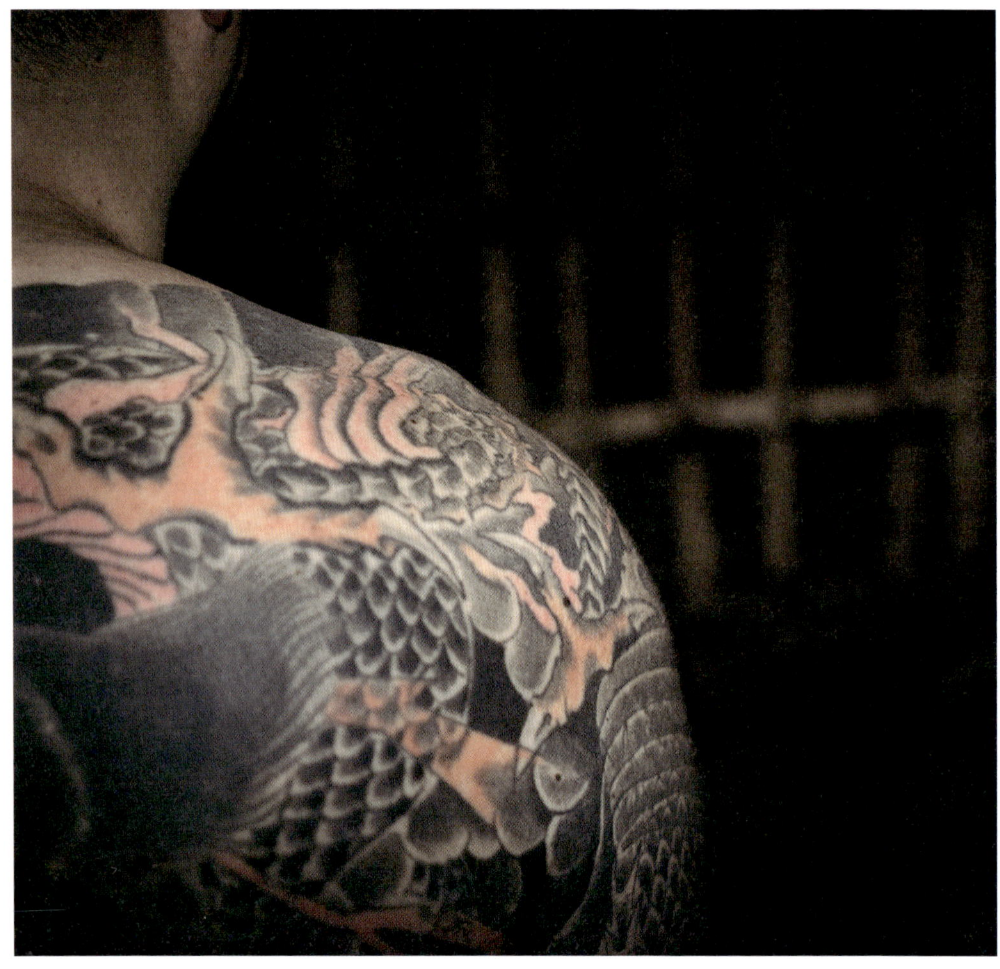

Yakuza member in an *onsen* bath house outside of Yokohama.

an opportunity to ask the members about the details of their tattoos, and as we looked at the pictures together, symbols were explained to me. The camera became my bridge for communication. I was there to do a job. This, combined with the fact that I had a key informant, a yakuza boss who informed everyone of what I had come there to do, allowed me to gain access to the yakuza.

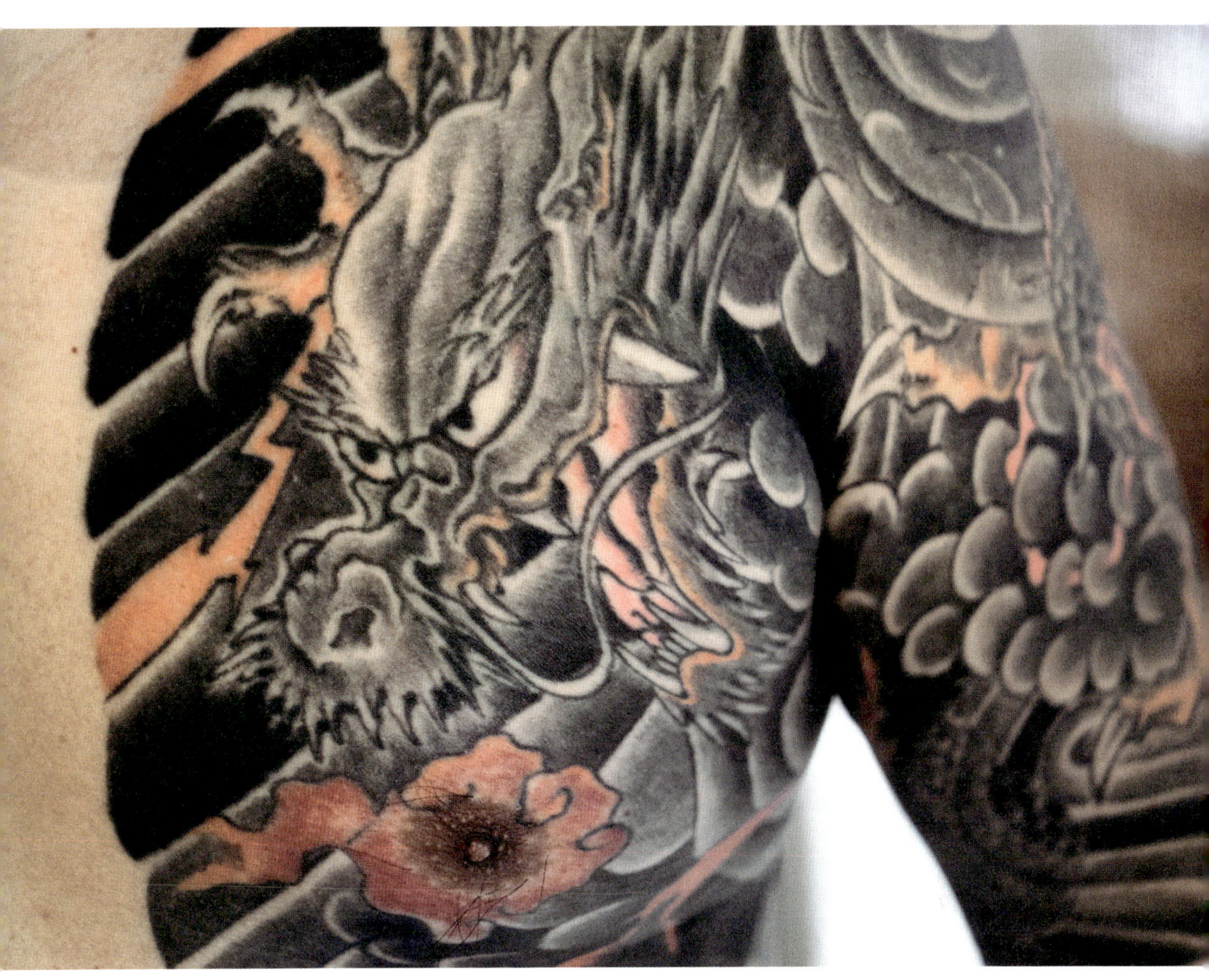

Close-up of a dragon *irezumi* with thunderbolt patterns.

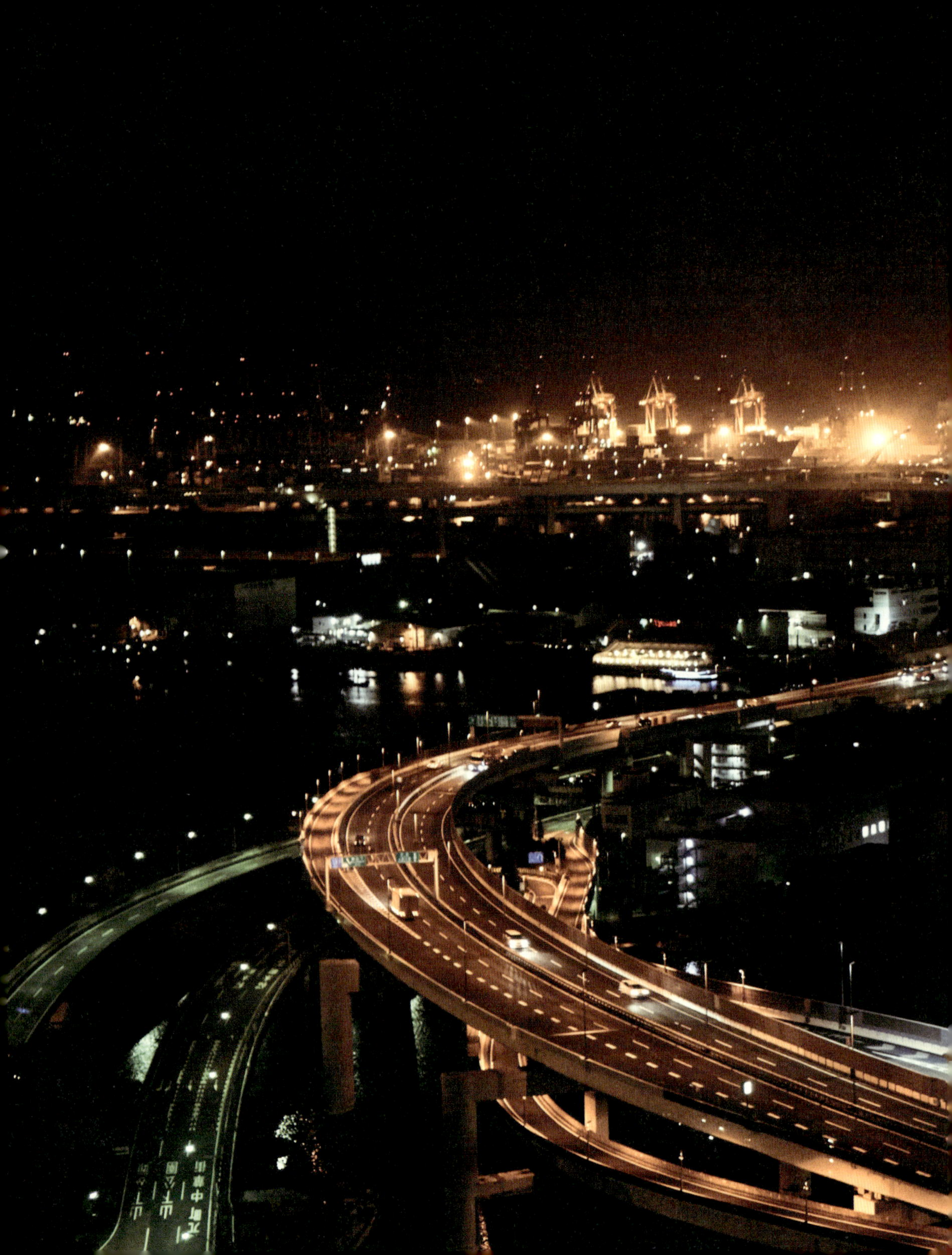

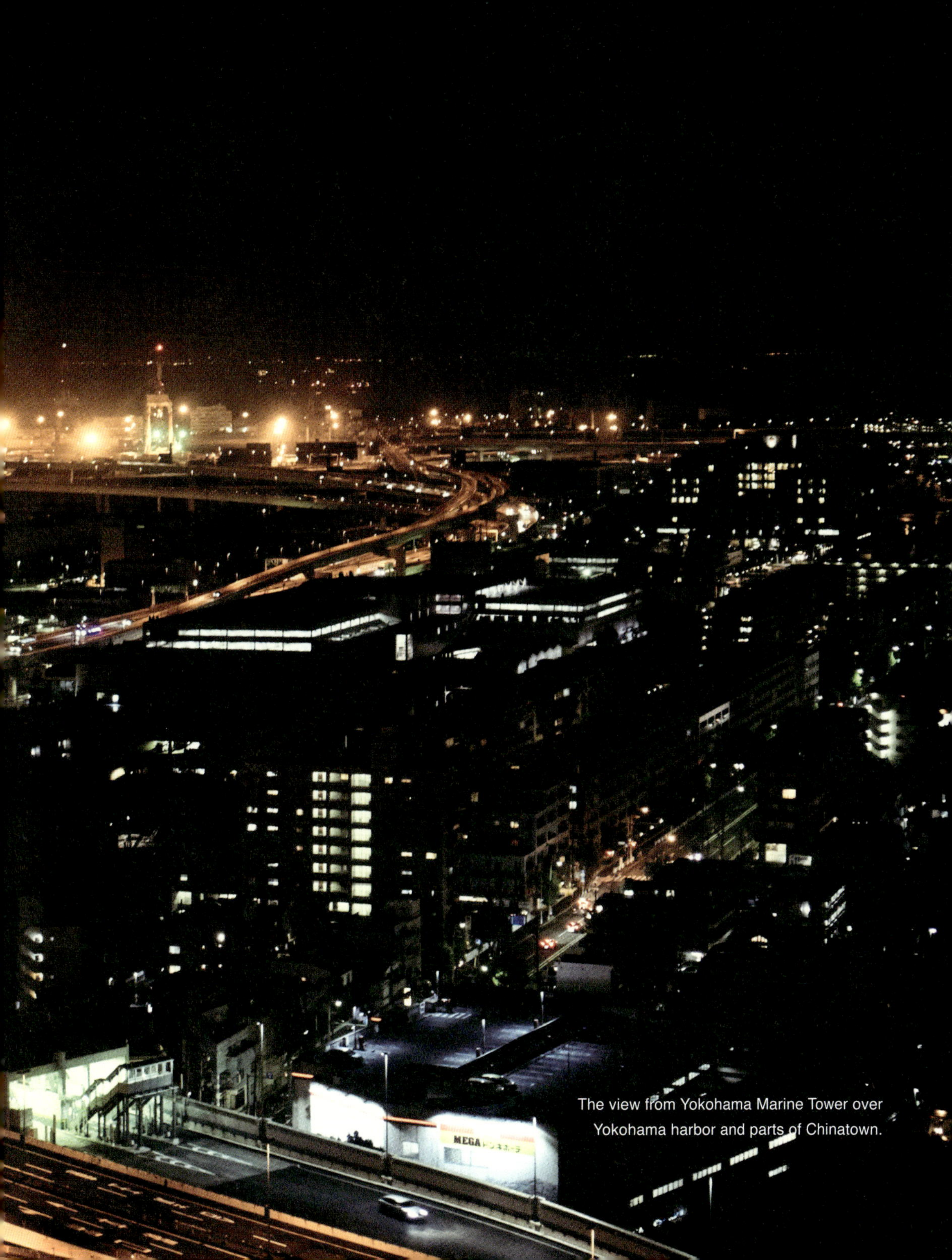

The view from Yokohama Marine Tower over Yokohama harbor and parts of Chinatown.

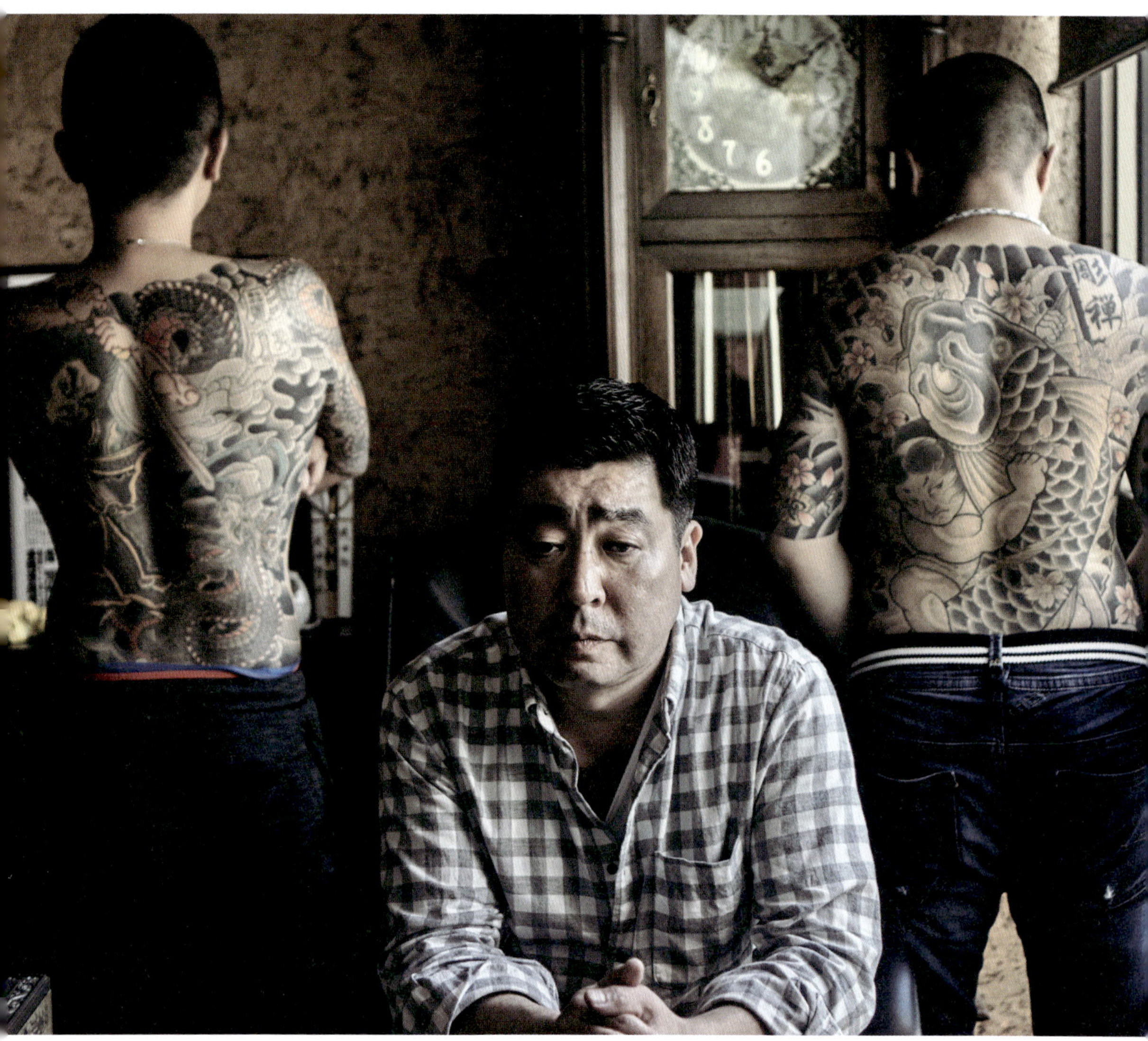

At the boss's office with two of his closest associates.

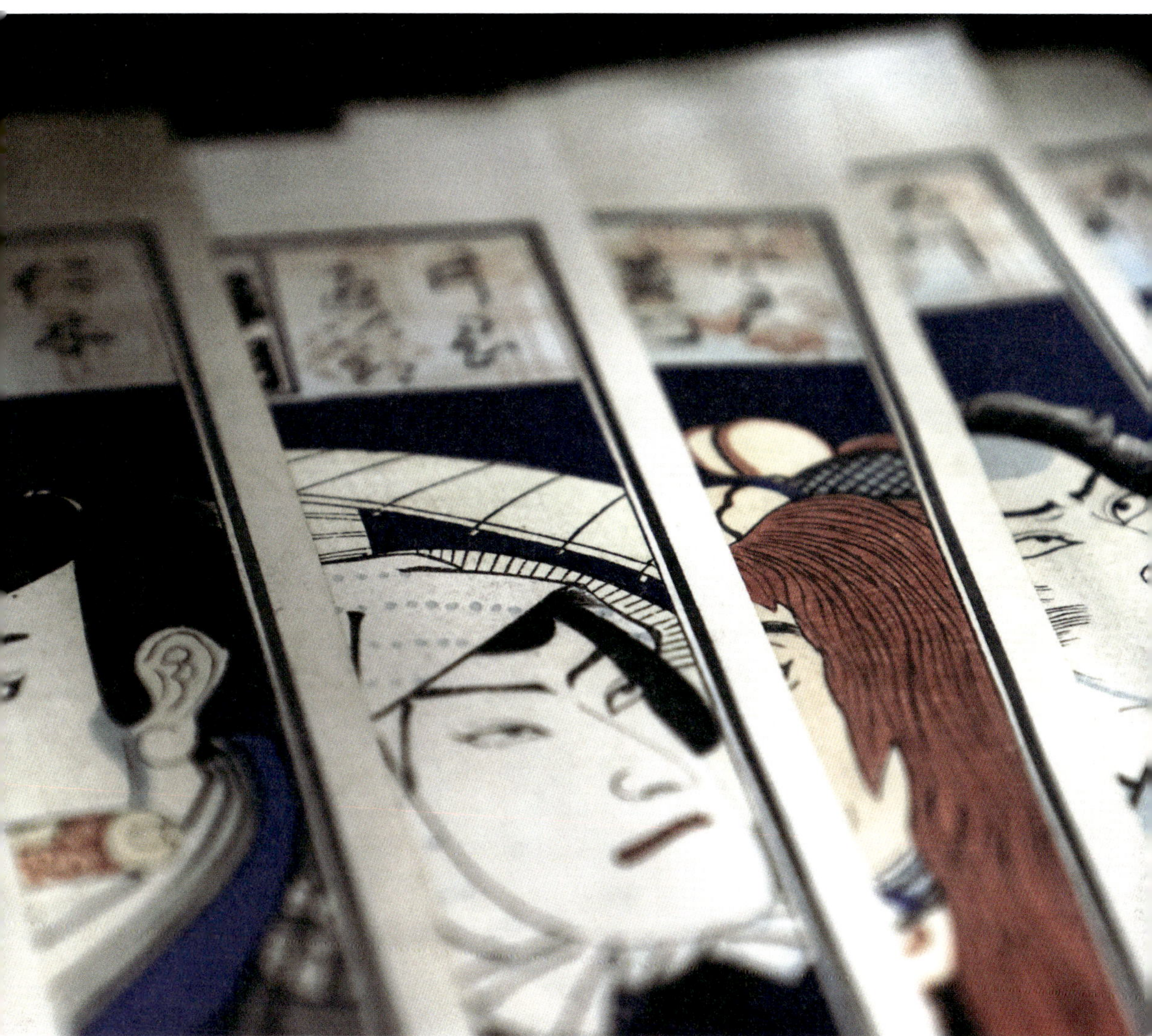

Cards featuring old kabuki actors in *irezumi* master Horimitzu's studio.

Meeting The Yakuza

To walk side by side with a boss from a yakuza family feels strange. As we walk through the dark alleys of Yokohama, some people bow while others look away when we pass them. I get the impression that even the birds are afraid to fly when they see one of Yokohama's infamous men.

I visited Japan in 2014 in order to present a paper at an international conference. Since it was my first time in Japan, I took some days off to explore Yokohama's tourist sites. One night, while sitting in a bar, I started to chat with the locals, and we talked about my field of research. I spoke of my interest in Japanese tattoos and the way symbols were used in the world of organized crime. One of the bartenders told me that he knew a good yakuza that I could interview. Since it was five o'clock in the morning and I had been drinking absinthe for the last hour, I asked him to arrange a meeting with one, and he did. I woke up the next morning with a vague feeling that I was to meet with a yakuza the same day. A few hours later, I went to the bar where we were sup-

posed to meet, and that was where I met Ken-San for the first time. Ken-San is a member of Masuda-gumi, but he is also a boss in his own family. I explained my interest in documenting Japanese tattoos. He opened his shirt, exposing his dragon *irezumi*, and said, "Why don't you start here?"

The photographs in this book were taken in Yokohama, a neighboring city to Tokyo. It is famous for its port, its Chinatown, and also for being one of the first cities to open up to the West after a period of national isolation. My material was collected at many different venues related to the yakuza, such as their headquarters, *onsen* (bath houses), and bars. I also visited Ken-San's home.

In 2015, I revisited Japan. Just hours after I landed at Narita International Airport, a black van was waiting outside my hotel. One of the side-doors swung open, and the words "nice to see you again" drifted out from inside the car. I snapped a picture with my camera, but I was very nervous. On entering the car, I could not help thinking that I might have just taken my last picture.

After a short car ride, we arrived at a restaurant. The yakuza explained to me that I came at a very sensitive time since the Yamaguchi-gumi were busy dealing with an internal conflict. My timing, therefore, was not the best, but one yakuza pointed out that it would be good if I tagged along, bearing in mind the sweatshirt I was wearing. I glanced down at the design on my chest and realized that the logo looked like a dartboard, which made me a perfect target. The others, who were sitting around a table covered in alcoholic beverages and nice food, laughed hysterically. I sipped my beer and smiled a little while my thoughts nervously turned to Atsushi Mizoguchi, an author who was stabbed for having written a book that put the Yamaguchi-gumi in an unfavorable light.

It was during my second encounter with the yakuza that I was offered an opportunity to take some photographs. Very few people in the world have been granted the degree of access that I have been granted in the last few years. Before my second visit to Japan, I believe I was quite naïve as to just how easy it had been for me to secure the access I needed in order to collect this material.

Even though I felt nervous and uncomfortable in the beginning, the relationships I formed with the yakuza I photographed and interviewed became very relaxed, especially when it came to the boss, Ken-San. He and the others treated me very respectfully, even though I slipped up a few times with regard to proper Japanese etiquette. I was told that I was being treated as a very important client, or even a "family" member, and that was the way I felt throughout this project.

If you do a Google image search using "yakuza" as the key word, you will not only find pictures of tattoos, but also a lot of pictures of men wearing suits. I traveled to Japan with this preconceived idea only to find that the yakuza I met did not ususally wear suits. Inspired by American gangsters, wearing a suit became popular among the yakuza after World War II. In the family I visited, suits were worn only at official business meetings. Some yakuza now wear modern western clothing. The sneakers, tracksuits and hip hop-influenced clothes they often wear make them more difficult to spot. Some of my informants expressed a desire to blend in and not be recognised "as yakuza all the time". As one member put it, "I love wearing hip hop clothes. As a matter of fact, I don't like wearing suits at all, but if you want me to, I can put one on and look scary for you." The cousin of the stereotypical gangster in a suit, the yakuza with a pompadour haircut, also haunts the realms of popular culture. In reality, this figure is seldom seen. Appearance is important, however, so when suits are worn, the bosses go for quality. Yakuza also wear expensive jewelry that become showpieces in their everyday lives.

The cars they drive and their office buildings also stand out in Japanese society. Most of the vehicles I saw were black luxury models with tinted windows. The office buildings have a bunker-like feeling with small windows and a single door, and security cameras surrounding the whole structure. Inside, there are offices, training rooms and bedrooms for recruits as well as meeting rooms decorated with fine art and family emblems.

Besides the clothing and tattoos, another prominent symbol among the yakuza is *yubitsume*. Members are often missing parts of their fingers due to the practice of *yubitsime*. *Yubitsume* literally means finger-shortening, and it often refers to cutting off part of your little finger. The practice can be done several times on multiple fingers, and it is most commonly done as an apology to the boss when a serious mistake has been made. If a subordinate makes a mistake that affects another family, for example, the boss can offer an apology by cutting off part of his finger in order to resolve the conflict. It was explained to me that if you make a really big mistake, you would have to cut off part of your thumb; that is the worst possible scenario. The practice was also explained as being a voluntary form of apology, although there are examples of people being forced to cut off parts of their own fingers. For instance, if a person left the yakuza with bad standing, they had to perform this action.

Members should perform *yubitsime* on themselves and present the finger to the boss – preferably attractively wrapped. If the boss accepts it, this indicates that he accepts the apology. Members I talked to had what struck me as a bizarrely relaxed attitude to this practice. Some of them laughed when they described how they did it, as it seems that the act of cutting off your own finger presents a set of practical difficulties. But

why do they do it? According to one historical explanation, losing the tip of a finger made it harder to use a sword, which meant that the yakuza would have to rely more on his boss's protection.

Despite the historical background, this appears to have become less common. When it is done, however, the boss is supposed to save the finger he has accepted. There are several reasons; one important incentive for not doing it is visibility. In Japan, if you happen to have a cut-off finger it is almost certain that you are, or have been, a member of the yakuza, and this will attract the attention of the police. Since *yubitsime* has been widely practiced, the prosthetics industry has developed accordingly, and there are now companies that specialize in making prosthetic fingers for active and former yakuza so they can either hide their pasts or blend in more easily in public.

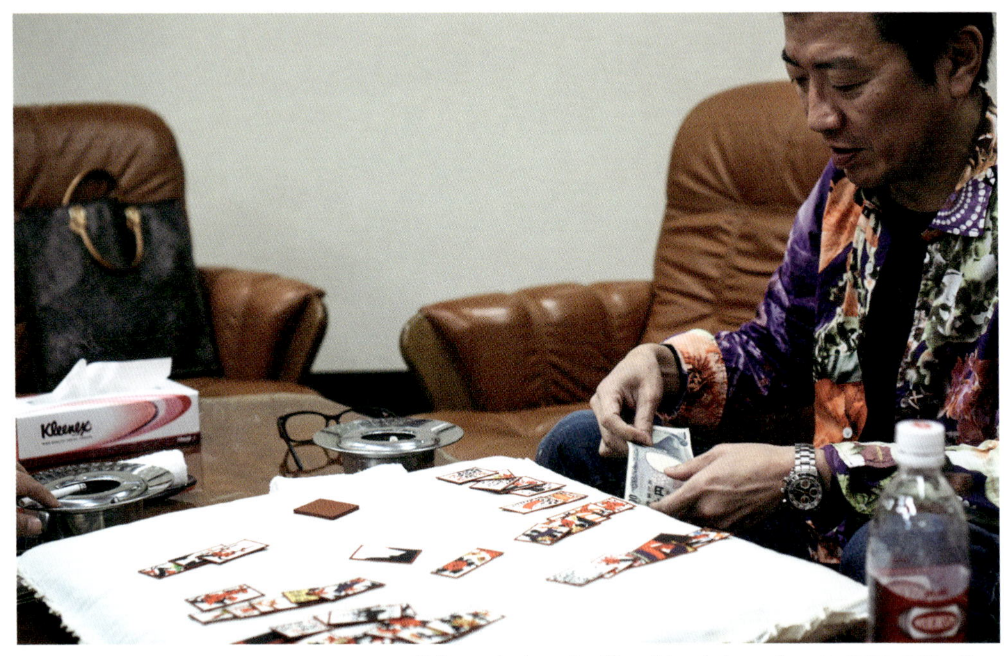

Yakuza playing a traditional *hanfuda* card game at the main office.

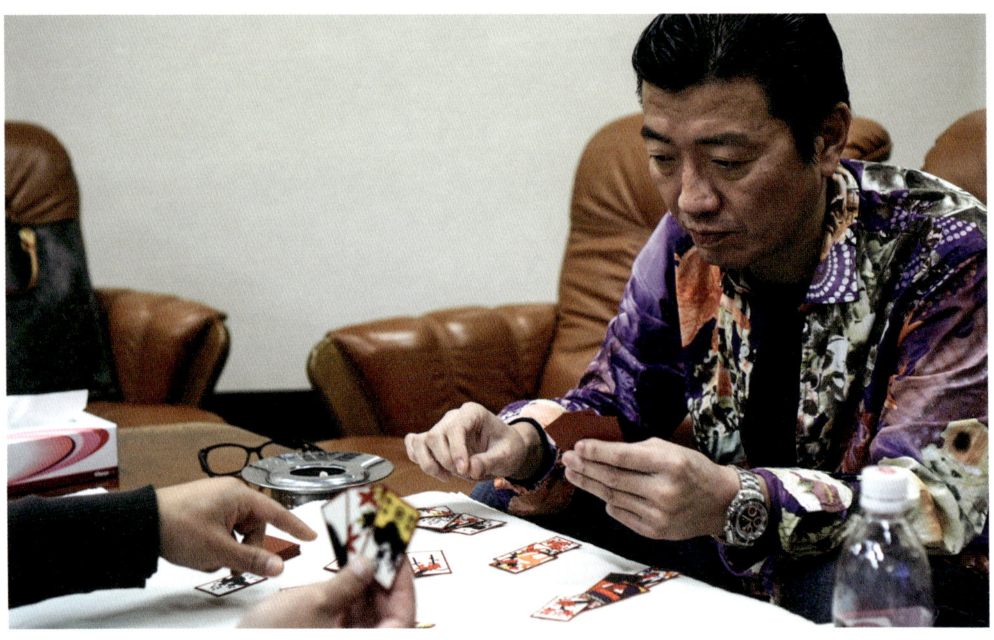

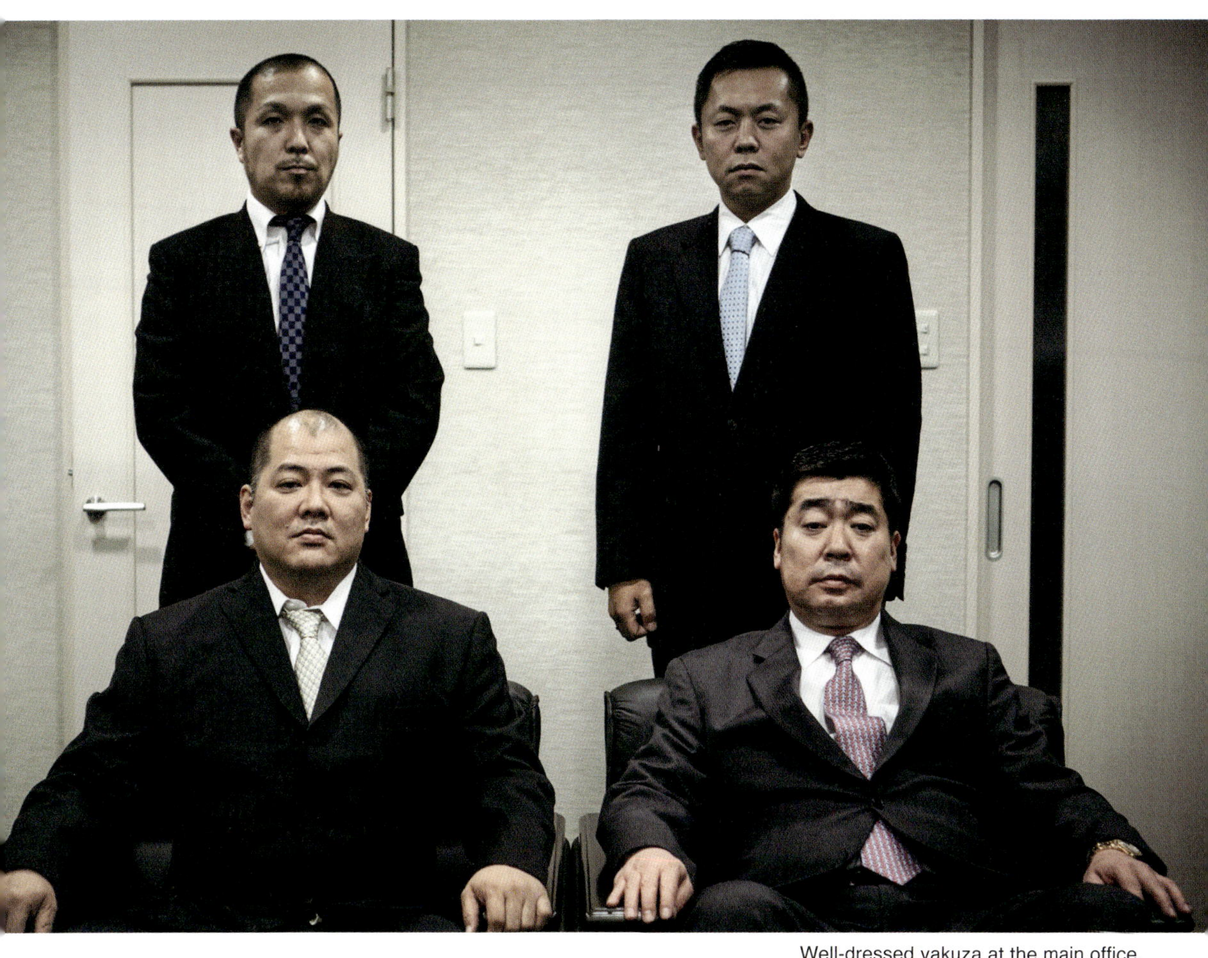

Well-dressed yakuza at the main office.

*As you can see, our cars are very expensive.
Why do we have these kinds of cars? We have them to show that
we have made it, that we can do anything. We want to impress
ordinary people so they feel that maybe they can do this too.
It's the same with clothes, jewelry, watches, shoes
and everything.*

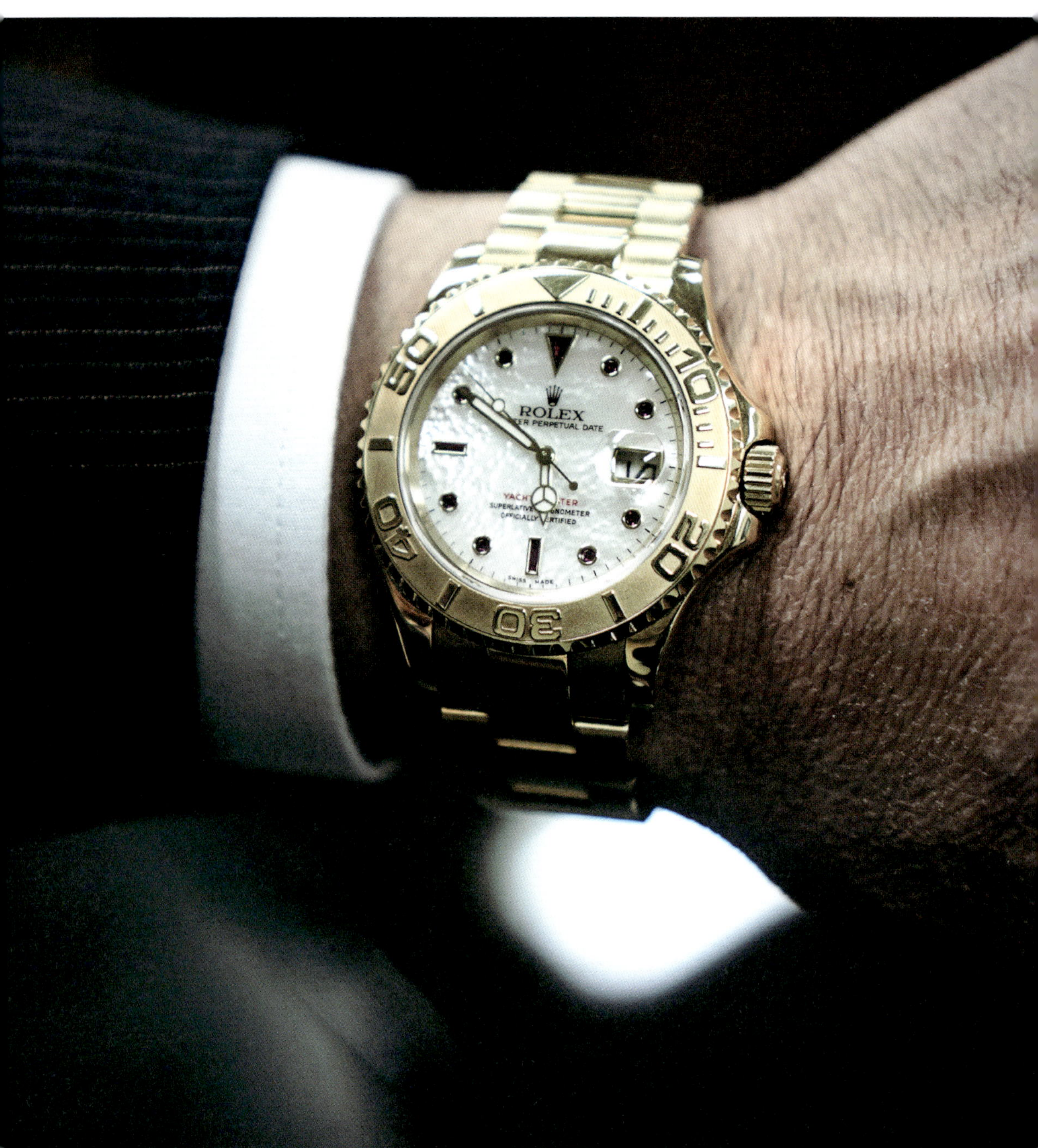

A Rolex belonging to a yakuza, a gift from his former boss.

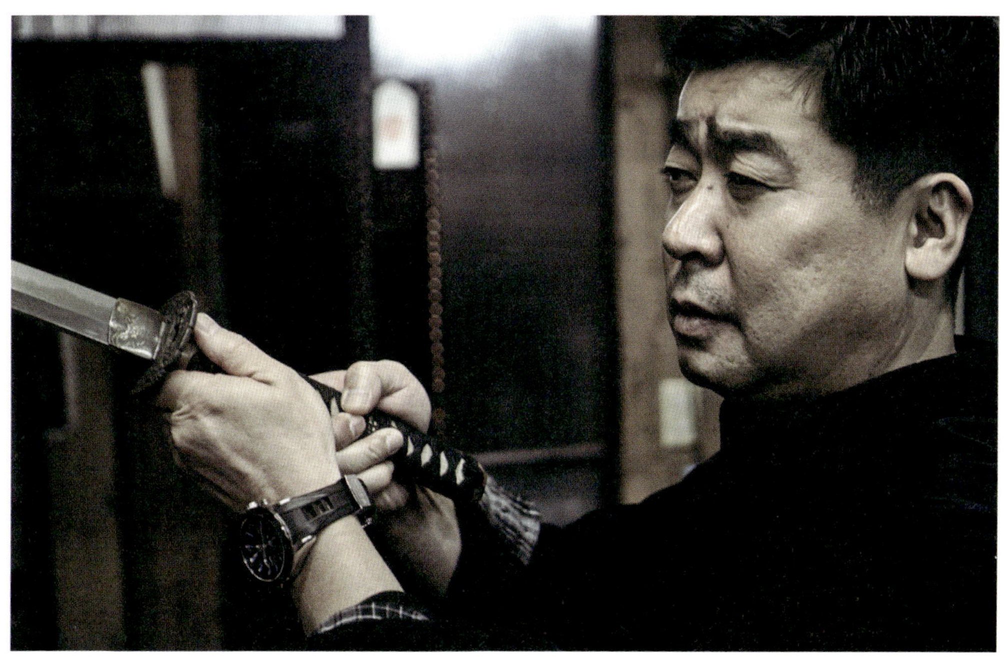

Boss with an old *katana* (samurai) sword.

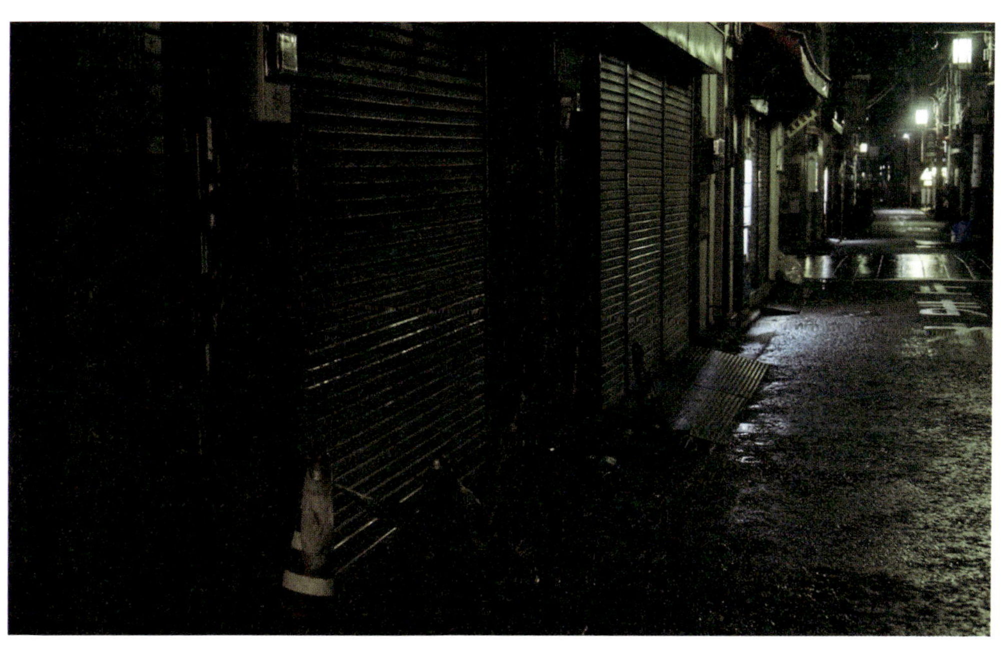

Alley in Yokohama Chinatown.

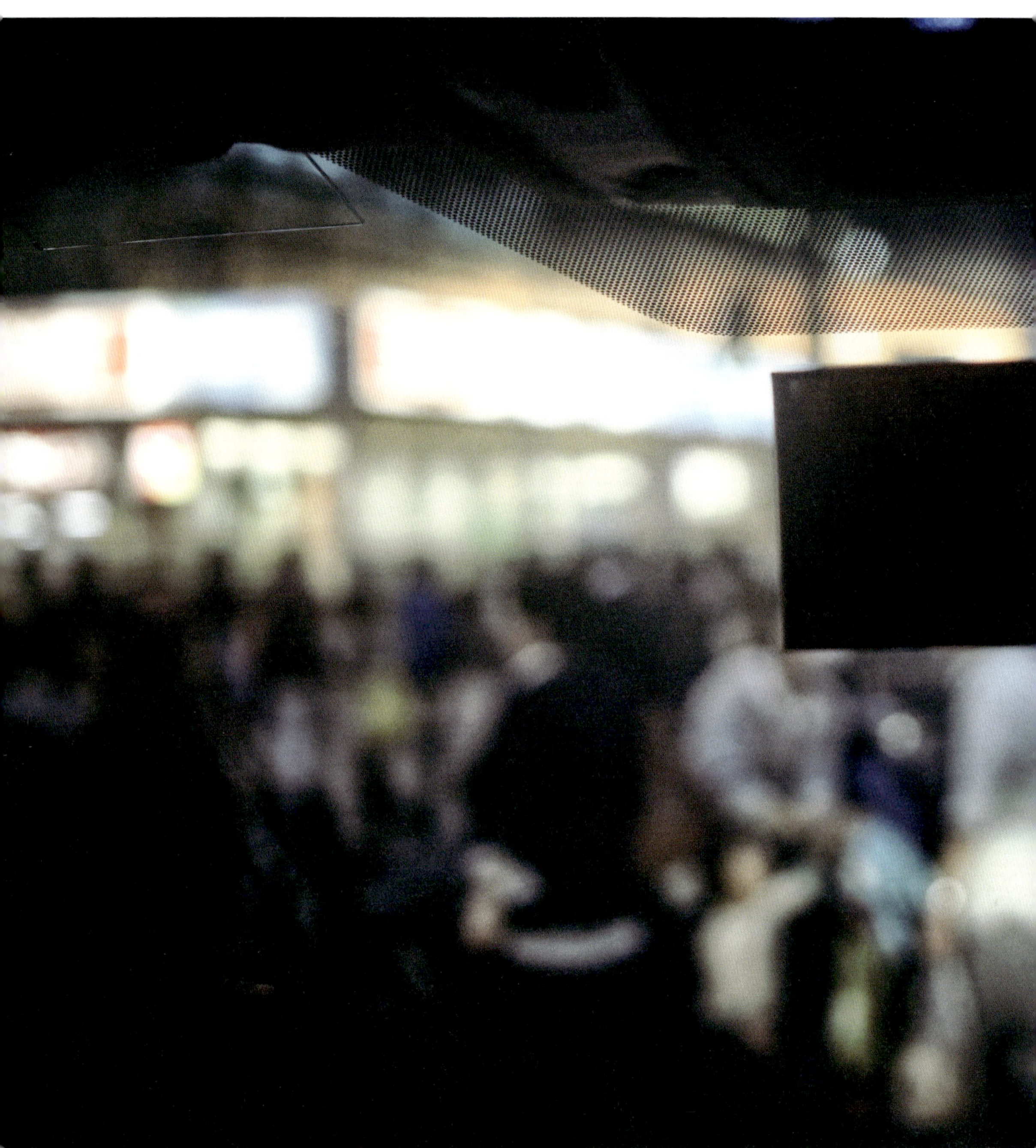

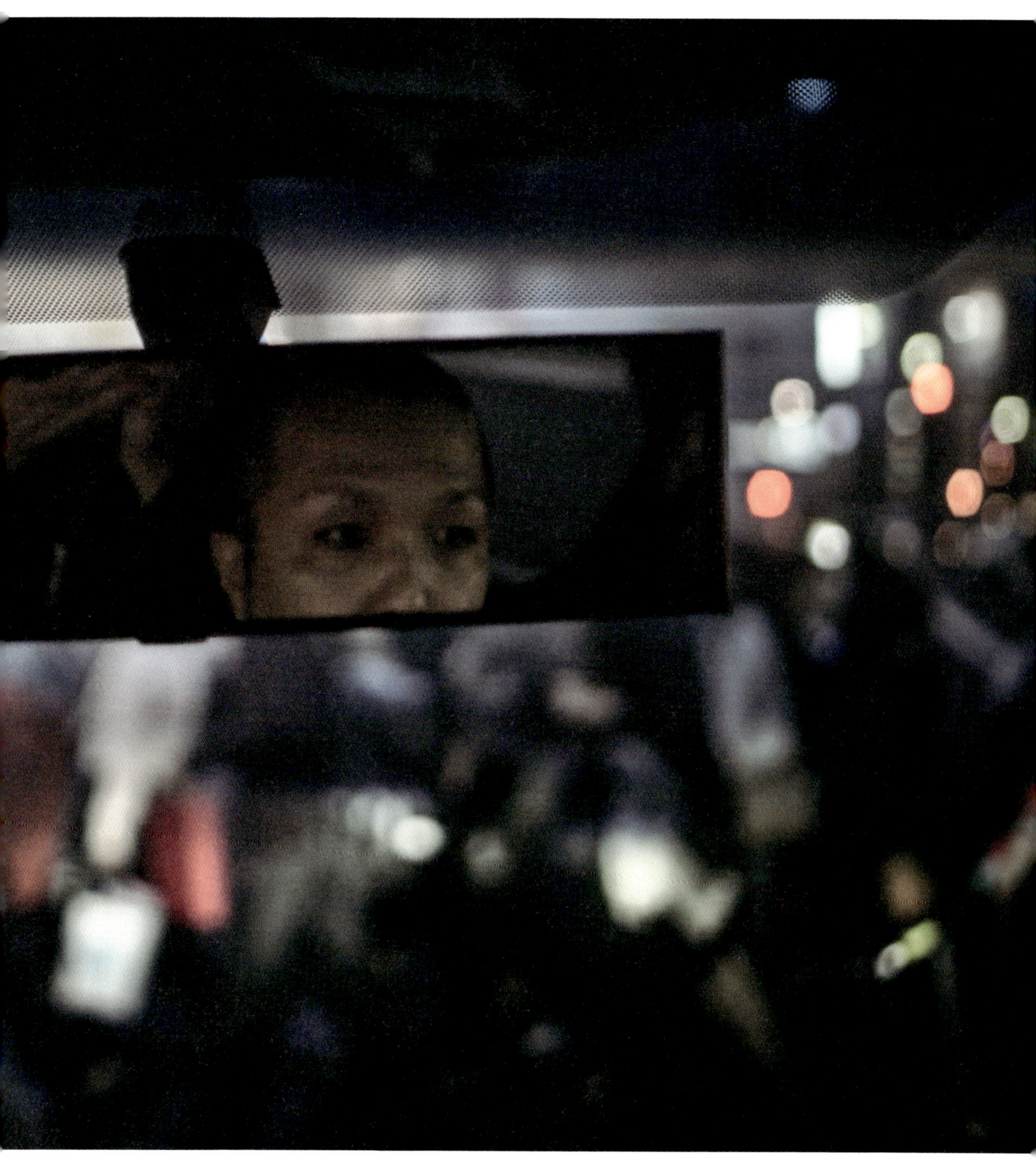

Yakuza driving the author across Yokohama.

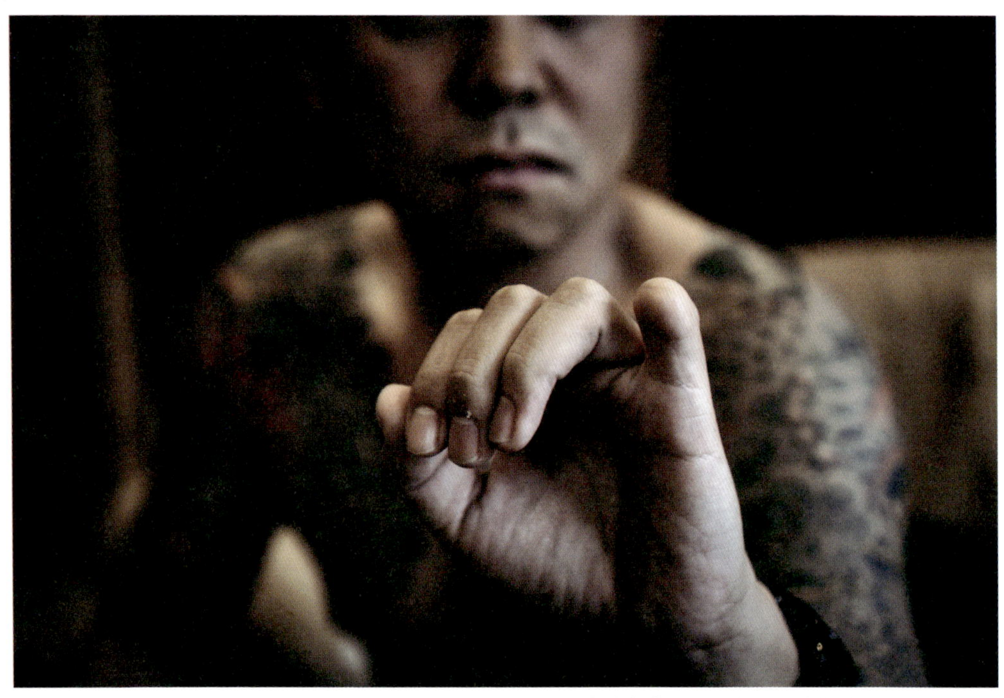

A yakuza showing his little finger while explaining how he cut it off.

*It was actually kind of funny since
it was tough to get it off. I used a hammer, and
while singing the Super Mario song I slammed down
the hammer and the finger flew away,
just like Super Mario.*

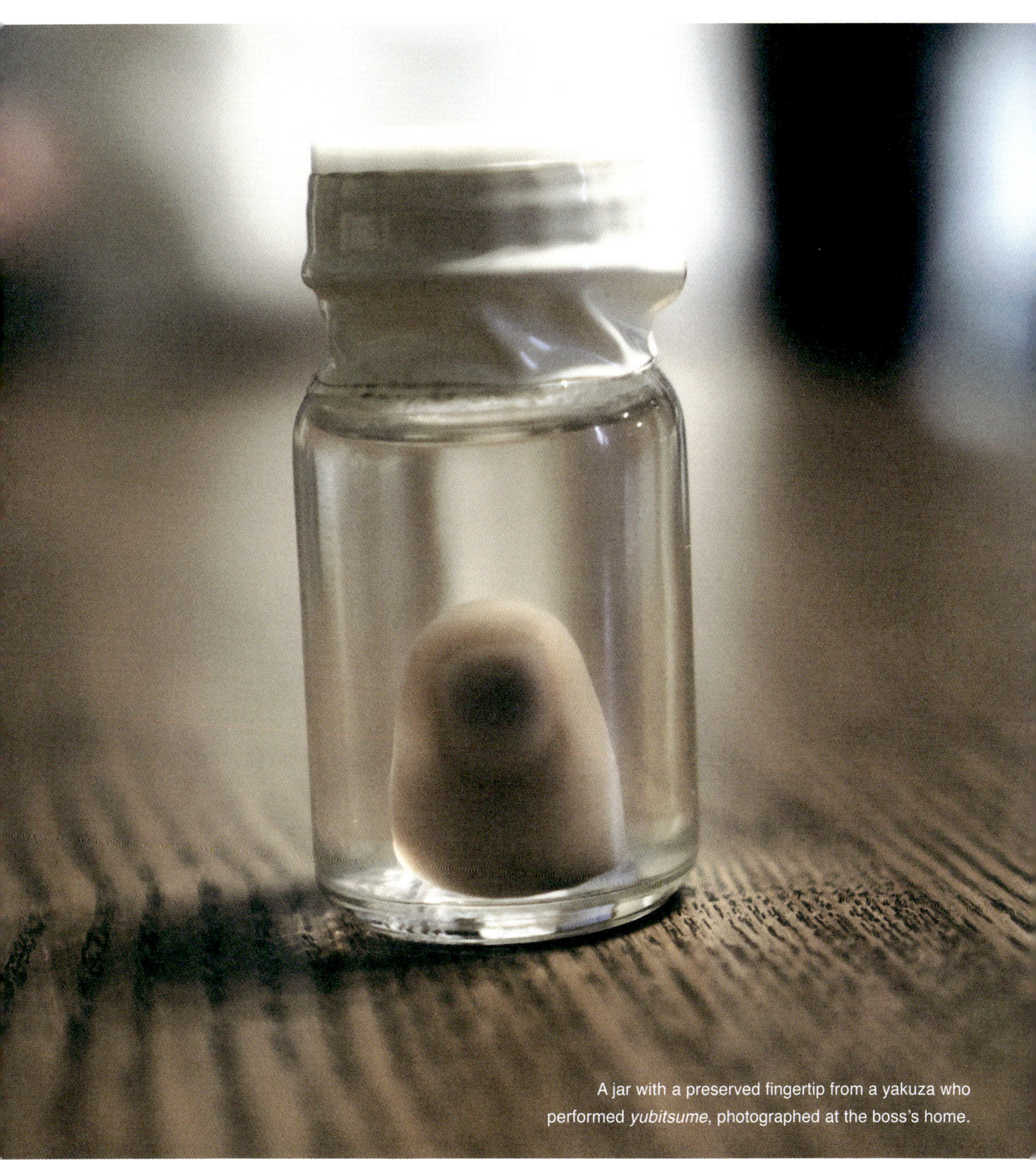

A jar with a preserved fingertip from a yakuza who performed *yubitsume*, photographed at the boss's home.

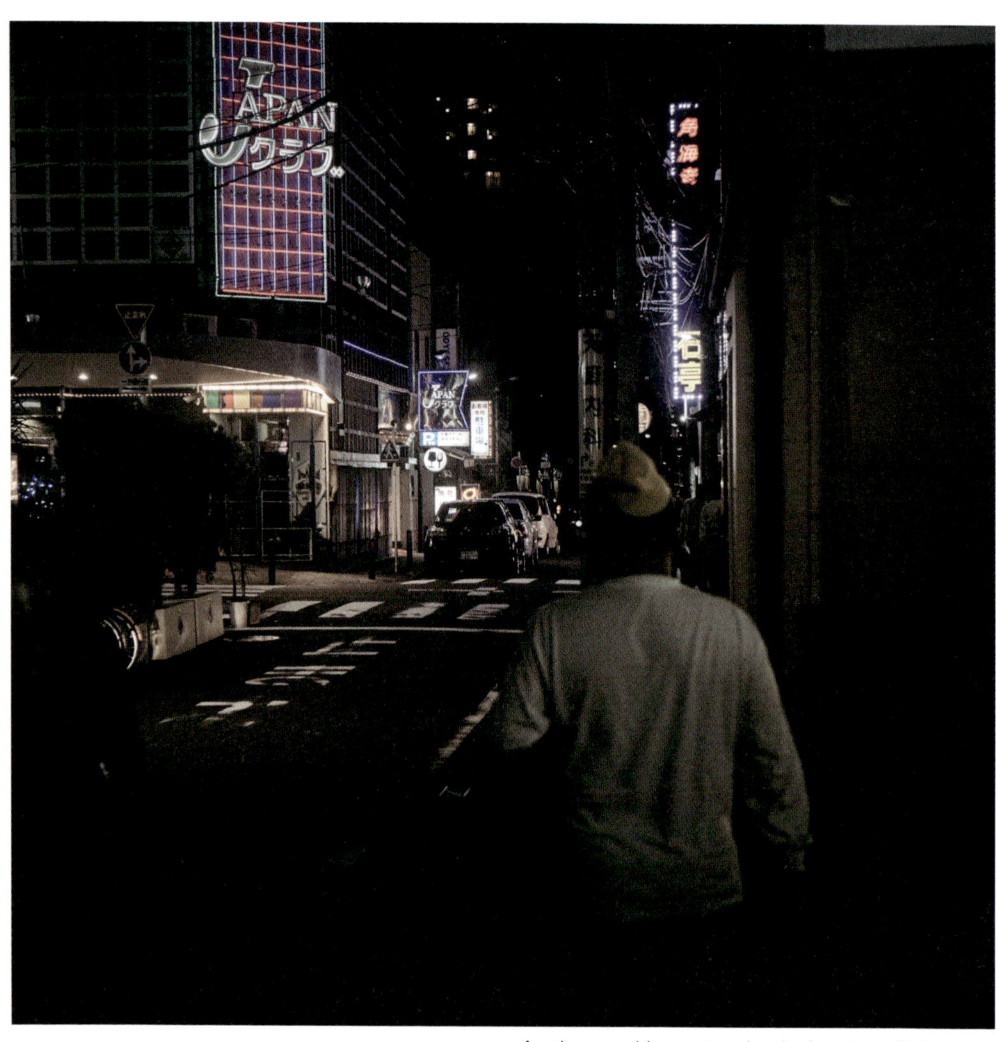

A yakuza on his way to a bar in downtown Yokohama.

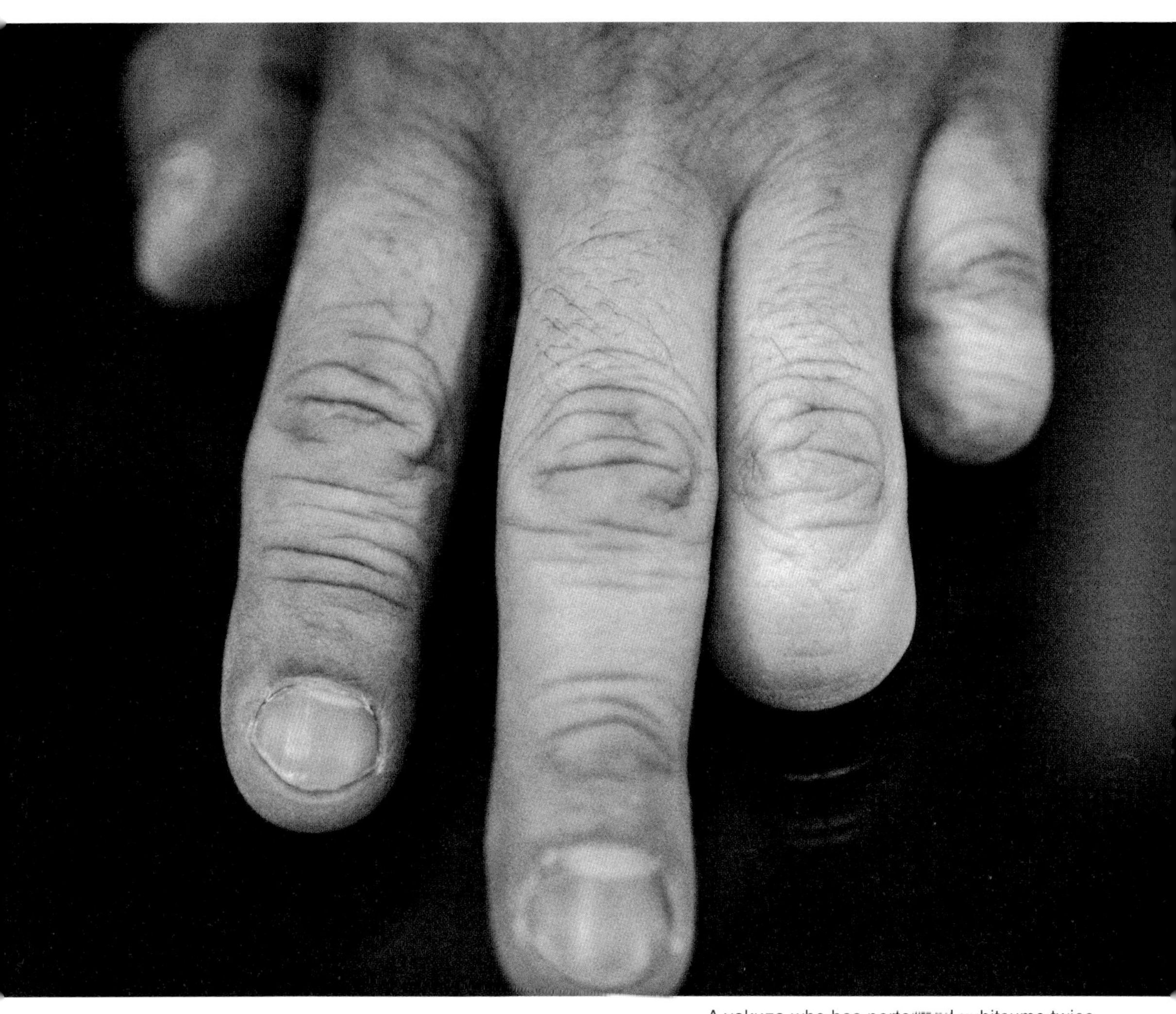

A yakuza who has performed yubitsumo twice.

Irezumi Masters & The Yakuza

An experienced *irezumi* master is treated very respectfully by both his apprentices and clients. Yokohama is the home of many famous tattoo artists, perhaps because it is a harbor city. One of them is Horimitzu, whom I visited along with some yakuza. As a sign of respect, they bowed very low when they met him. Like the yakuza, *irezumi* masters can belong to groups that have a family-like structure, and just like the yakuza, they were once considered to be an organization shrouded in secrecy. Rather than advertising their presence, they relied on the respect they received from their customers. For example, an *irezumi* master can assign his apprentice to his (there are very few female *irezumi* artist in Japan) *irezumi* alias. The *irezumi* master also seems to have a great deal of influence when it comes to whom he will work with and the motif. The master may have several meetings with a customer in order to read his or her personality before deciing on a suitable motif.

"It's not about the price, it's about getting a feeling for whether someone would actually like to have an *irezumi*. For example, if a customer wishes to have a specific irezumi on his body, I as the *irezumi* master, can tell him that it's better to have this one, it suits your personality better. So, you see, I offer advice. Sometimes people come with suggestions that are nonsense. I would never make an *irezumi* of that. They have to go elsewhere. If you don't have the time or the heart for an *irezumi*, you shouldn't get one. I used to do my tattoos only by hand, but nowadays I use a gun too. When it comes to the design, if the person hasn't decided what they want, but has a story, I will draw up a design that captures that story."

Horimitzu speaks with a great deal of integrity and authority when he talks about his work. He makes it clear that there is a huge difference between what he does and the creations of an *irezumi* artist that does more western-style tattoos. An *irezumi* is like a spirit. I was told by both Horimitzu and the yakuza that this is why the *irezumi* master chooses a motif so carefully. Horimitzu explains that there is more meaning attached to the traditional *irezumi*. Nowadays, *irezumi* have in some respects entered the realm of fashion, but he would never accept to do one for that reason. The person must be in it for the whole spiritual experience. Some yakuza also made it clear to me that the design itself is important.

What is also typical of *irezumi* is that they cover much of the body with one image. The backgrounds on Japanese *irezumi* are black and grey. Depending on the nature of the image, the background might consist of shadows, clouds, waves, water, mountains or thunderbolts. These backgrounds also make up symmetrical patterns on the body and are combined with different symbols. Flowers, for example, are common features. Cherry blossoms represent a "burst into bloom, and fall all too soon" approach to life because they are short-lived. The process takes many hours to complete and is extremely painful. One yakuza told me that "it took more than 200 hours over the course of two years, and I will probably do more." However, there is more than one way of doing it. Perhaps the most traditional process involves tattooing the upper part of the body like a suit, with the back and arms covered (to varying degrees) as well as the chest, except for a part in the middle, so that a kimono can be worn without the risk of exposing the *irezumi*. The legs are also covered (to varying degrees), and sometimes even the genitals. The motifs

are balanced. For example, if an upward-facing dragon appears on one side of the body, it will often be paired with a downward-facing dragon on the opposite side.

Today, *irezumi* artists in Japan vary in terms of the tools they choose to use. Many of those who do traditional motifs use both tattoo guns and the *tebori* technique. *Tebori* takes years to learn and gives the *irezumi* a different appearance, which many prefer to the result produced by a gun. Some *irezumi* masters, on the other hand, only use a gun, even when working on traditional designs. Another aspect of the traditional Japanese *irezumi* culture is the ink, or *sumi*, which is mixed from scratch by the master or his apprentice.

Background patterns and Ken Takeda, the name of the boss, tattooed on a yakuza's leg.

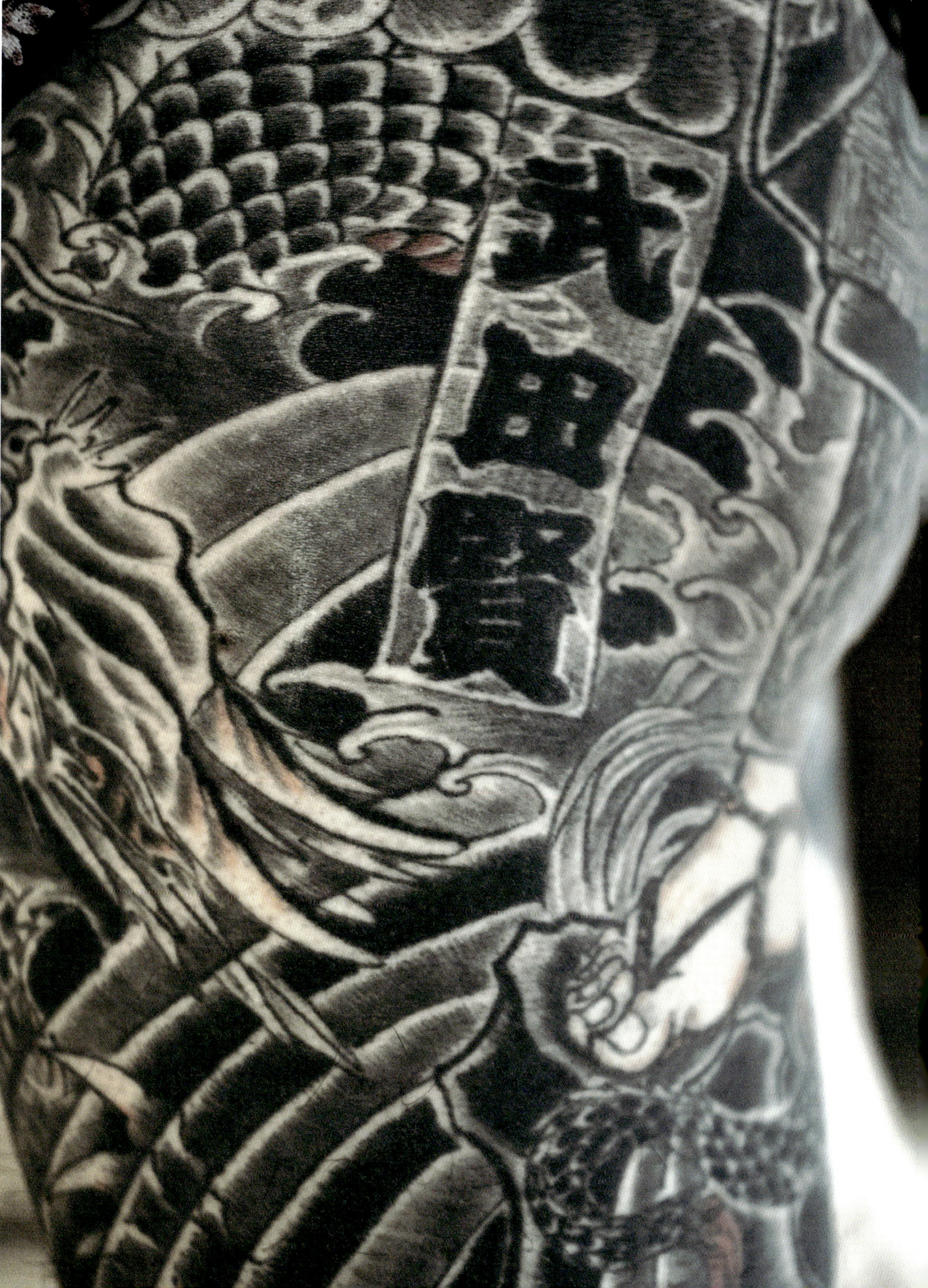

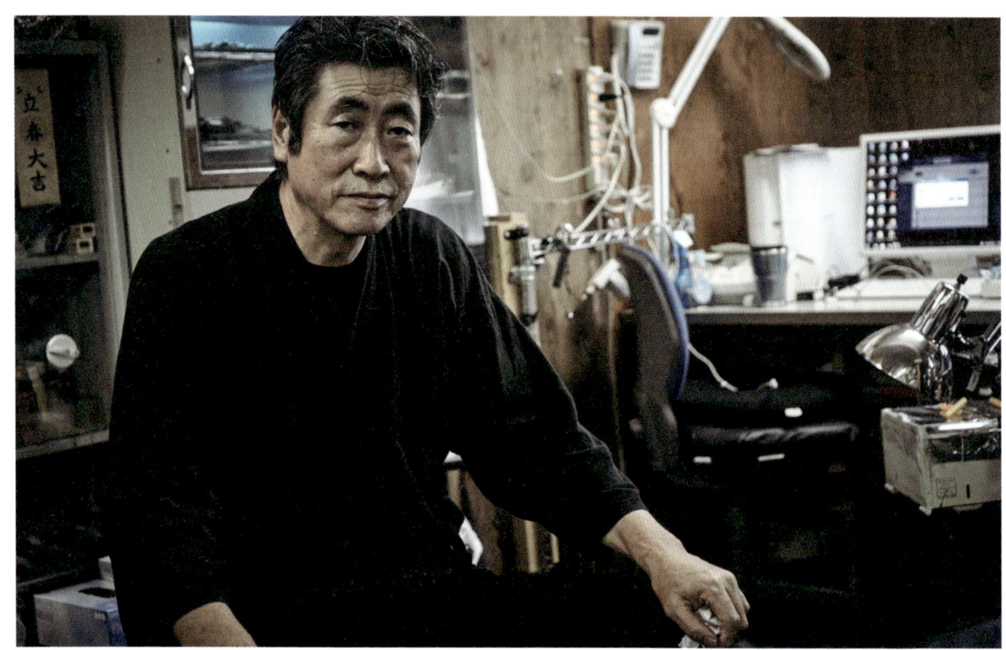

Irezumi master Horimitsu in his studio.

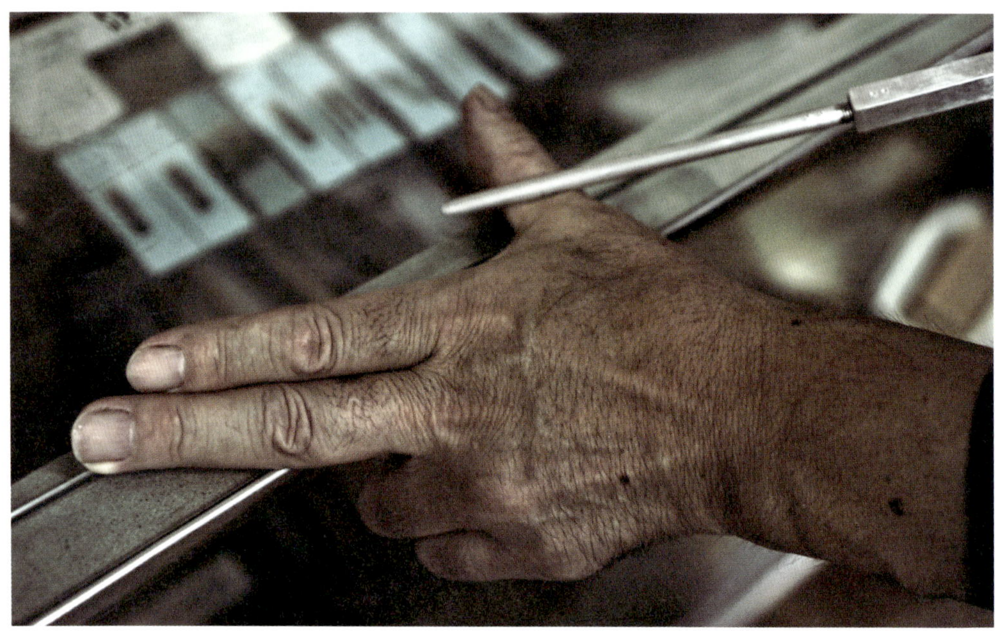

Horimitzu is showing the rod used for traditional *tebori*.

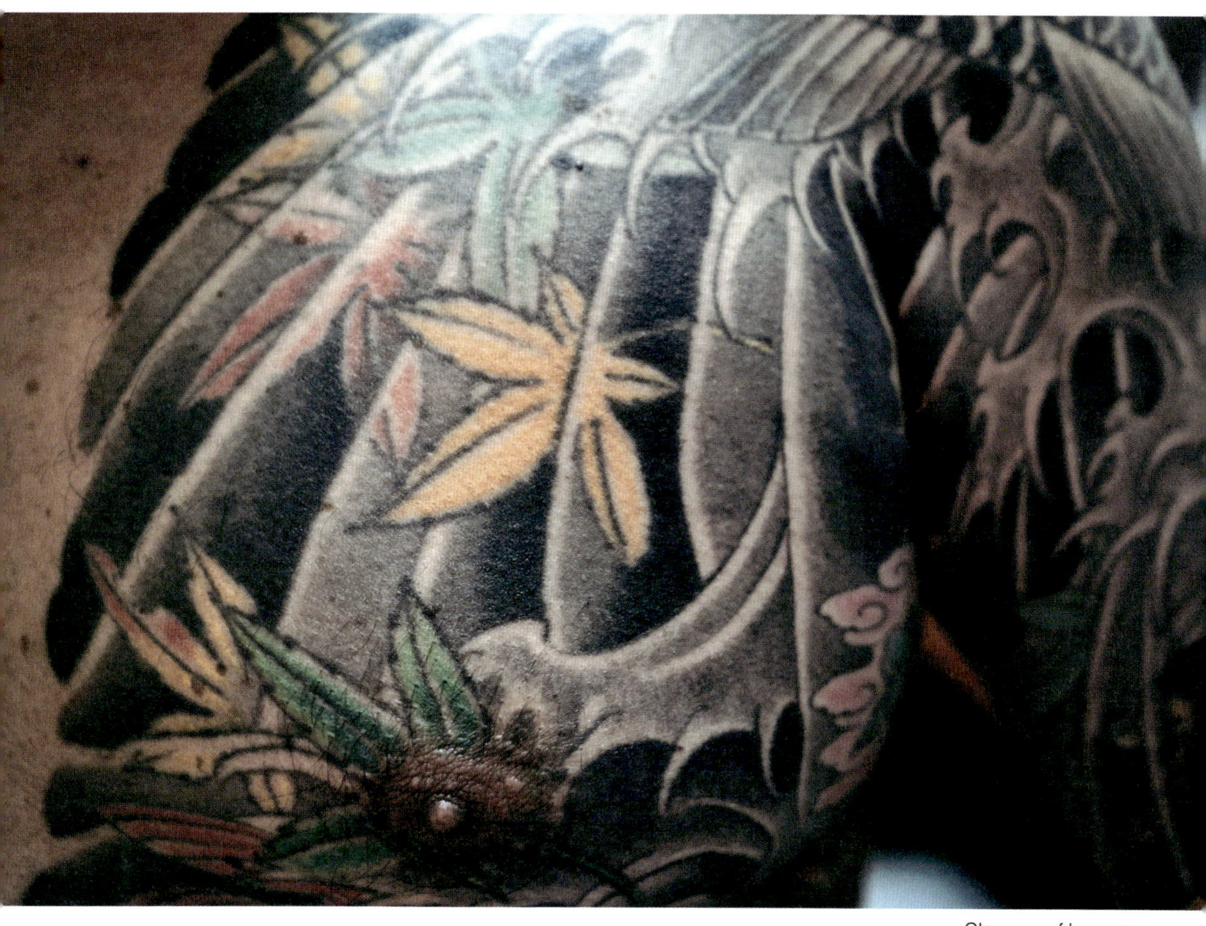

Close up of leaves.

Getting an irezumi is to dirty your body,
the body that your parents gave you. But doing
it as a yakuza is to say that you will never return
to a normal life.

Goddess on the back. Kannon. For me it symbolizes strength and power when fighting. My irezumi master told me that this is a powerful one, so if I chose it, it would be good for me.

Irezumi of the goddess Kanon
surrounded by a dragon.

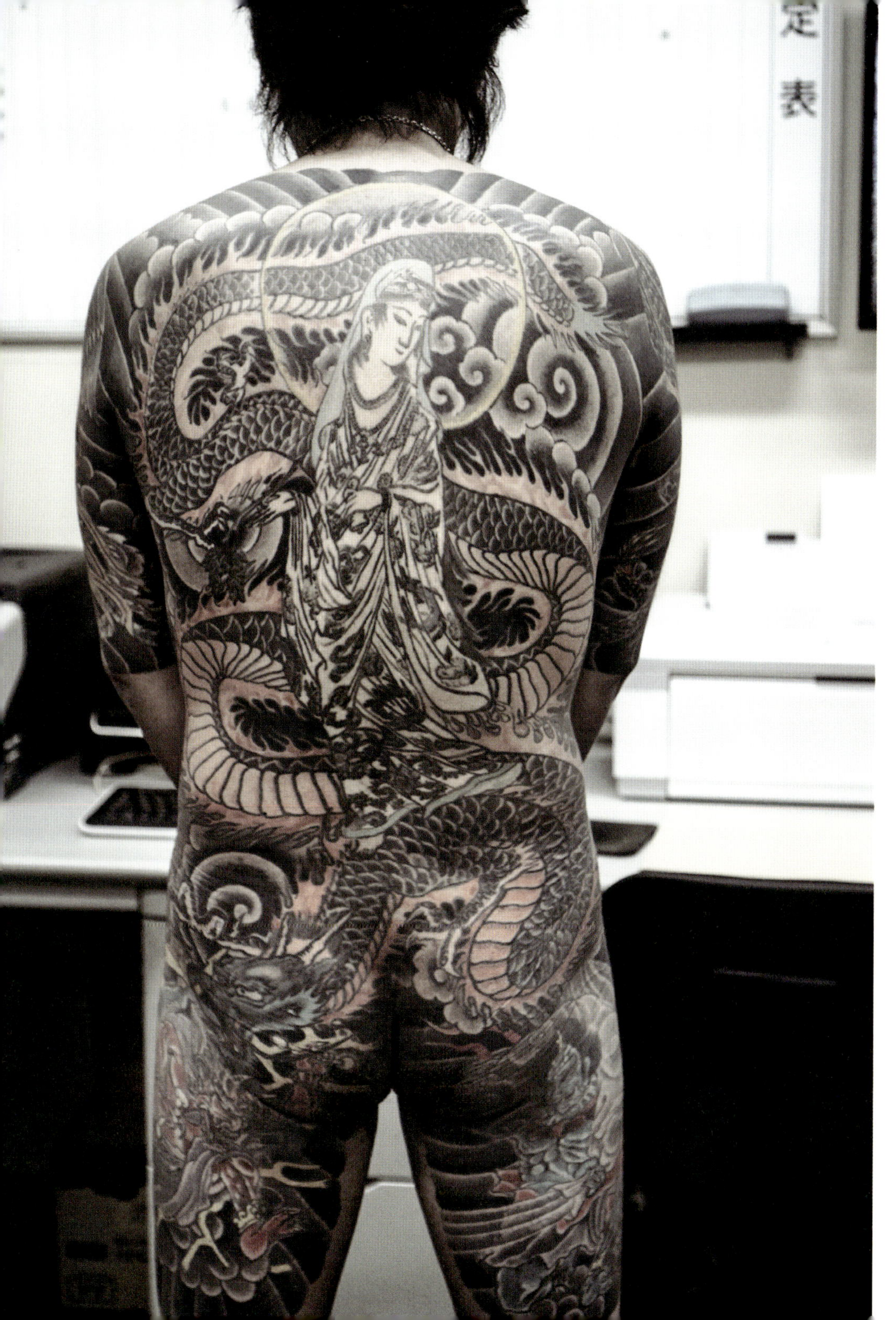

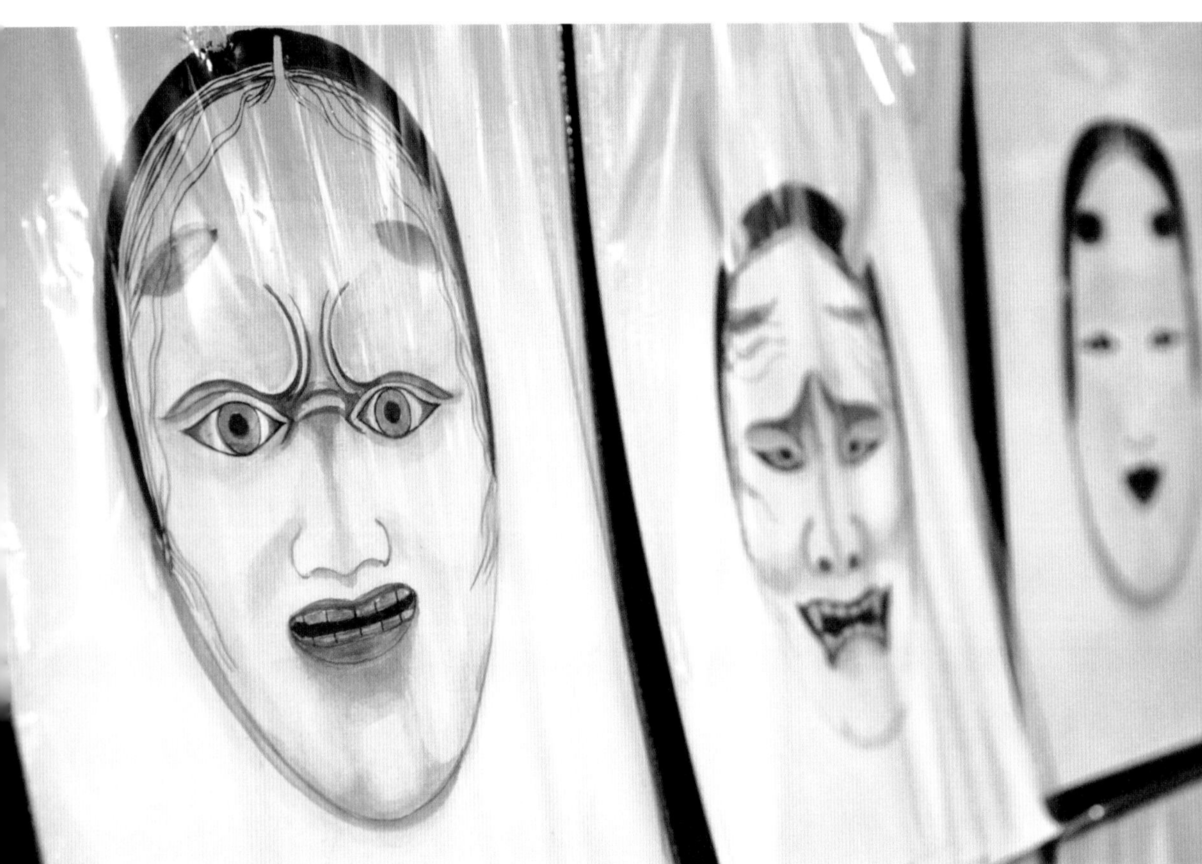

Hannya mask drawings by *irezumi* master Horimitzu
in his studio, Yokohama.

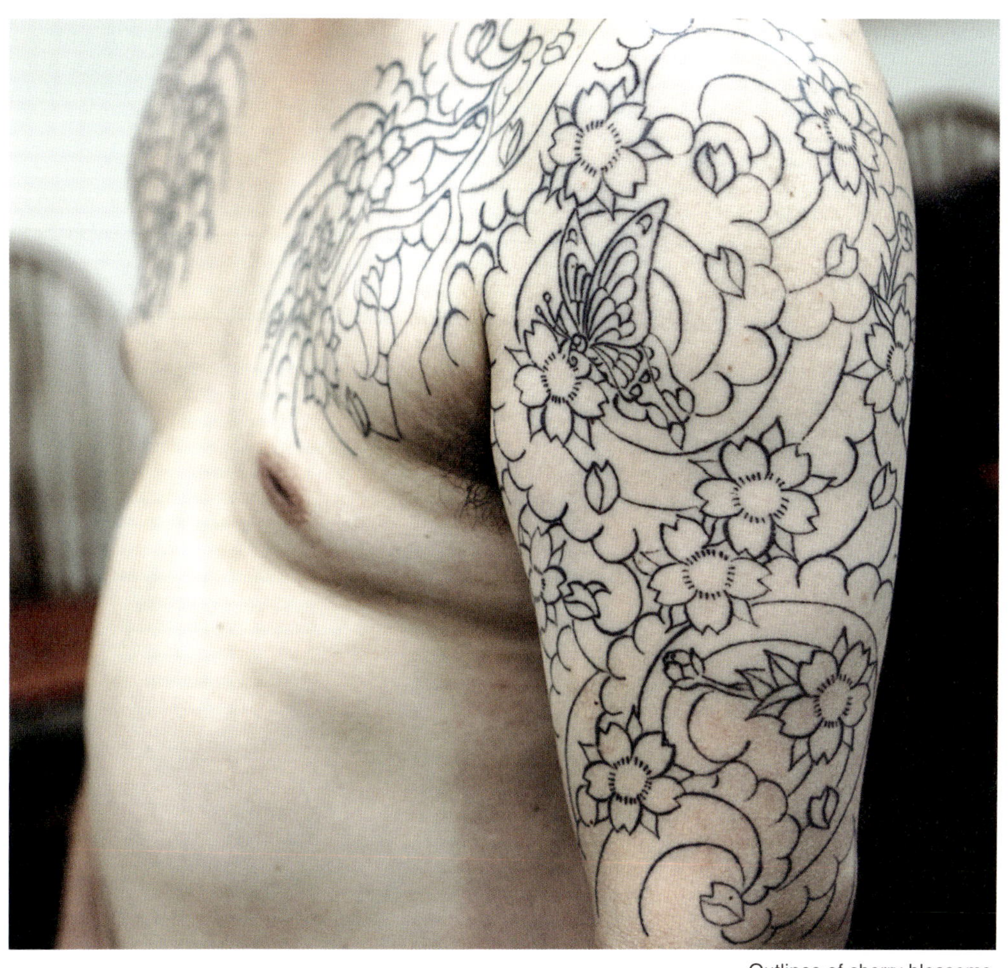

Outlines of cherry blossoms.

Just like cherry blossoms, our lives burst into bloom and fall all too soon.

Heroes & History

A common theme on yakuza *irezumi* is connected to the history of the organization, or rather its perceived history. No one knows when the yakuza came into being. It probably began to take shape in the Edo era (1600–1868). Its beginnings are said to be connected to gamblers (*bakuto*) and street peddlers (*tekiya*) of times past. This connection should not be understood as a linear process, but as a remnant of ancient customs. The concepts of *bakuto* and *tekiya* are even used by the police today when they categorize members of the yakuza. Historically, gamblers used dice or *hanafuda*, small cards with colorful patterns. It is in this context that we find the origins of the word "yakuza". One of the losing hands in the card game *oicho-kabu* is 8, 9 and 3, which is pronounced *ya-ku-za* and came to mean something similar to a worthless thing. The word also carries another meaning in that it can refer to an outsider or an unfortunate person, and it was adopted by the gamblers. As gambling was illegal in Japan, gamblers were marginalized in society. The word yakuza, as it is used by the modern organization, became popular after World War II. The street peddlers (*tekiya*) of the past who were also connected to the yakuza, were often seen at temples and shrine festivals. They combined selling substandard merchandise with entertainment and they used to trick their customers by, for example, selling counterfeit products and pretending to be drunk.

Members of the yakuza prefer to emphasize their connection to the samurai of ancient Japan. Samurai and heroes from traditional stories can be found in the *irezumi* of the yakuza. Although it is difficult to map the ties historically, it is clear that this is the way in which members wish to portray themselves. Their ideal is the romantic gangster, a kind of Robin Hood figure. The notion of the yakuza's noble past is also shared by non-members. The yakuza refer to their organization and way of life as *gokudo*, which means the ultimate way to many of them. The samurai group that Japanese historians claim the yakuza is descended from is the *machi-yakko*. They were ordinary men who lent a helping hand to towns and battled against the evil samurai of the shogun. The term *bushido* is referred to as the code of the samurai, connected to Japanese values of loyalty, generosity and affection for the weak.

The stories about the 108 outlaw heroes found in the Chinese novel *Water Margin* gained immense popularity in Japan, and they were illustrated by many artists, including Kuniyoshi. In his illustrations, some of the heroes get large *irezumi*, and this helped give a boost to *irezumi* culture in Japan. These paintings and stories live on in many yakuza members' *irezumi*. Two of the most famous characters from these stories are Kyumonryu Shishin and Kaosho Rochishin. The former is depicted with nine dragons tattooed on his body. The latter is tattooed with images of flowers. He is referred to as the flower monk, as he dons the costume of a monk in order to hide from the police. In one famous story, we find an illustration of these two heroes battling each other. They are ultimately forced to conclude that they are equal in prowess and therefore decide that the fight was a draw. After this incident, they become blood brothers. During the period when woodblock printing was developing, the illustrations to one particular novel, the *Water Margin*, had become very important for traditional Japanese *irezumi* culture.

Ninjas are another set of national heroes that you can find depicted in Japanese *irezumi*. Generally, as they are portrayed in the West, we think of them as being dressed solely in black, but not here. Ninjas are similar to samurai and have received excellent martial arts training. They are also reputed to have magical powers and can vanish into thin air. In Japan, you come across many legends about ninjas. Some of them have Robin Hood-like qualities (Ushiwaka, for example) and are portrayed in a fighting stance (defending the poor), which of course is well-suited to the yakuza-bushido ideal. Others are pictured sitting in a meditation pose (Ryuoh-Maru, for example), hands poised in a special position in order to channel energy.

Most yakuza come from problem homes challenged by, for example, poverty, and many are school drop-outs. I noticed this pattern in the lives of the members that I have met. The boss, for example, told me about the problems he had in school and why he later joined the yakuza.

Another interesting fact about the yakuza is that they have their roots in society's most impoverished groups, which includes some Japanese-Koreans and *burakumin*, or outcasts. These groups have traditionally had low status in Japan, and the *burakumin* have faced widespread discrimination; there are still reports of them being the victims of racism.

Money is a recurring theme when members talk about why they joined the yakuza. Most often, I heard them speak about growing up poor. In this regard, it seems that the yakuza I spent time with struggled with various difficulties early in life.

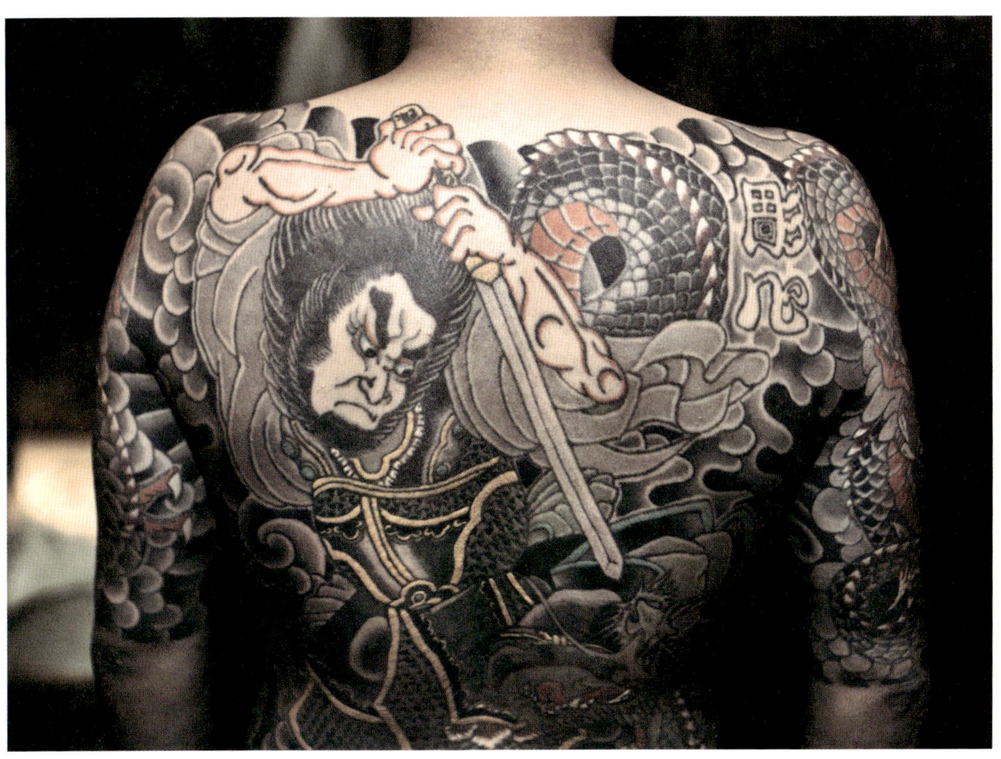

Teitoku Son, a hero from the *Water Margin* stories, battling a dragon.

We're sharing with people that can't afford to eat. It's the spirit of the yakuza to fight against the oppressor for the oppressed. We help the poor, and that's the difference between ordinary people and the yakuza.

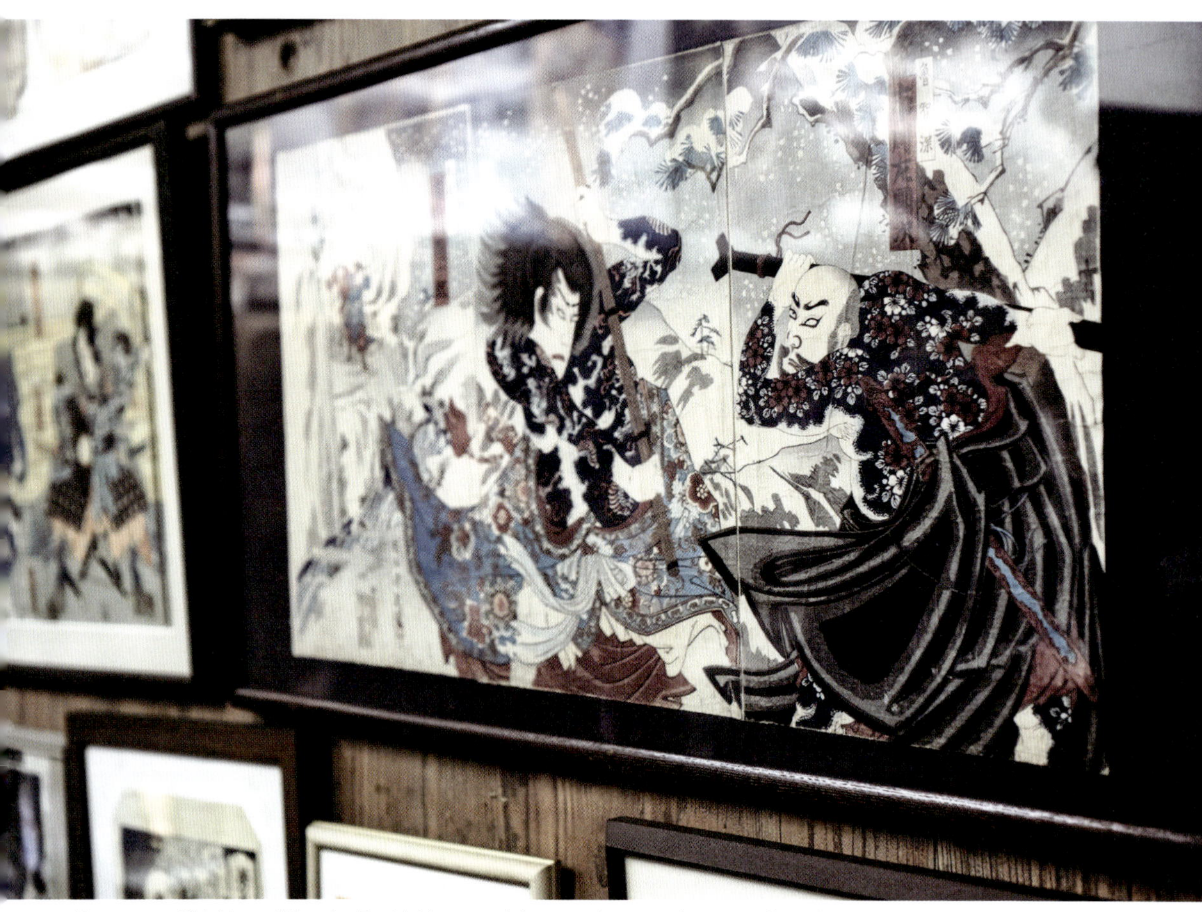

Kyumonryu Shishin and Kaosho Rochishin, two of the most famous characters from the
Water Margin stories, on an old wood print in *irezumi* master Horimitzu's studio.

One thing I need to say is that the yakuza is not a mafia. We are the yakuza. We have our special way. The yakuza spirit can be traced to the samurai way of life, bushido. These spiritual ways aretraditionally Japanese. The bushido spirit works for the name of the house. Even sacrificing his own fame and life. Other warriors may die for themselves, but the bushido spirit is about consideration and sacrifice for the family name.

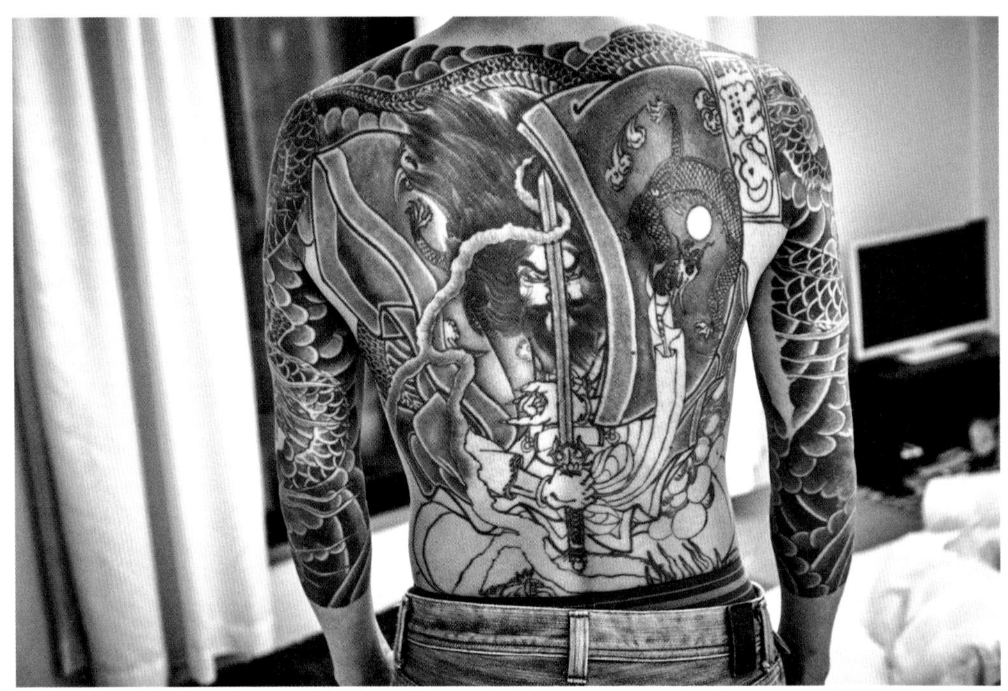

Kou Son Shou, a hero from the *Water Margin* stories.

We are the yakuza. We know that we're considered bad, but we're not bad people. We take care of the bad people that are under our control.

Hanfuda cards, associated with gamblers (*bakuto*) and the origins of the word "yakuza".

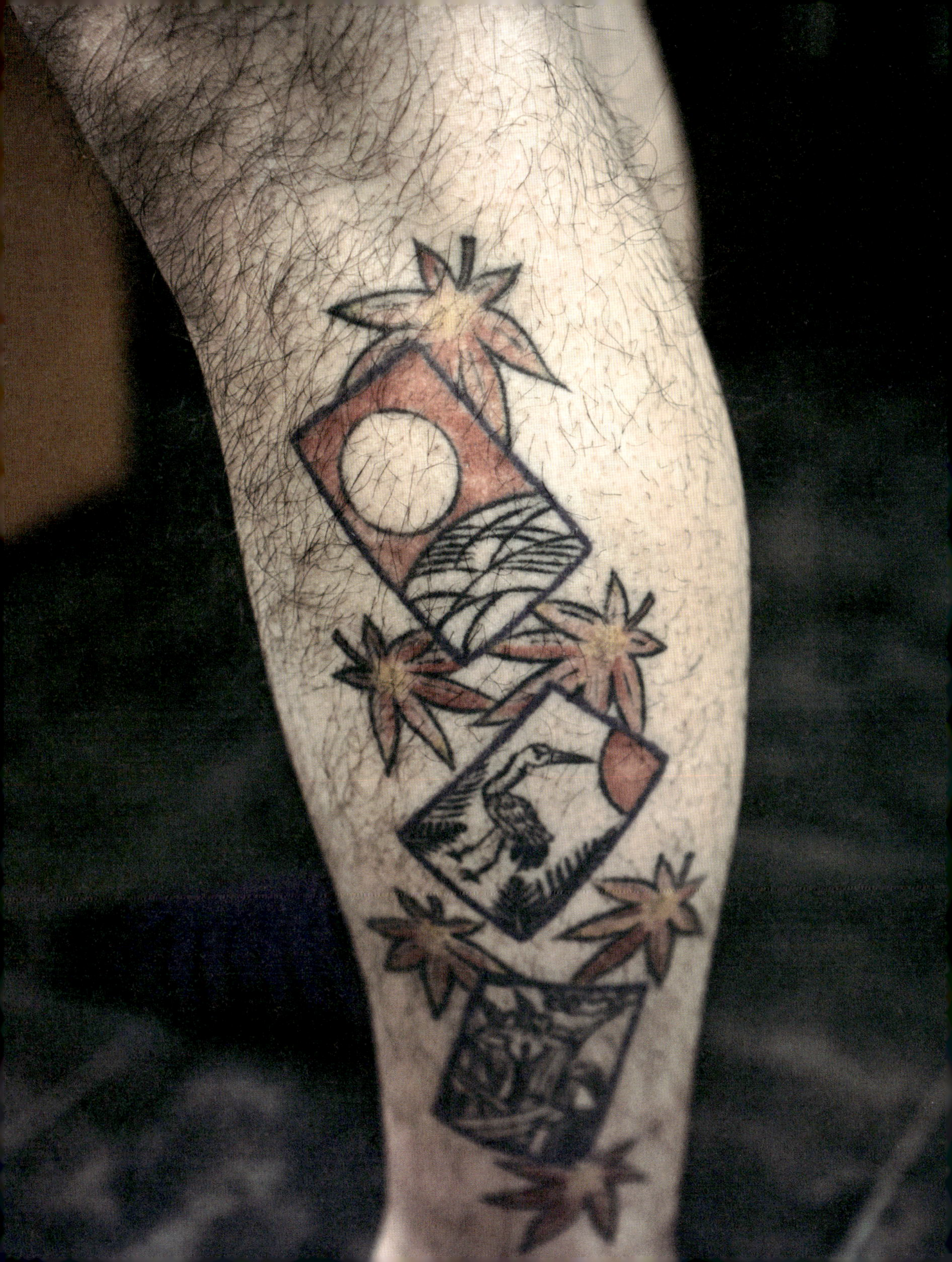

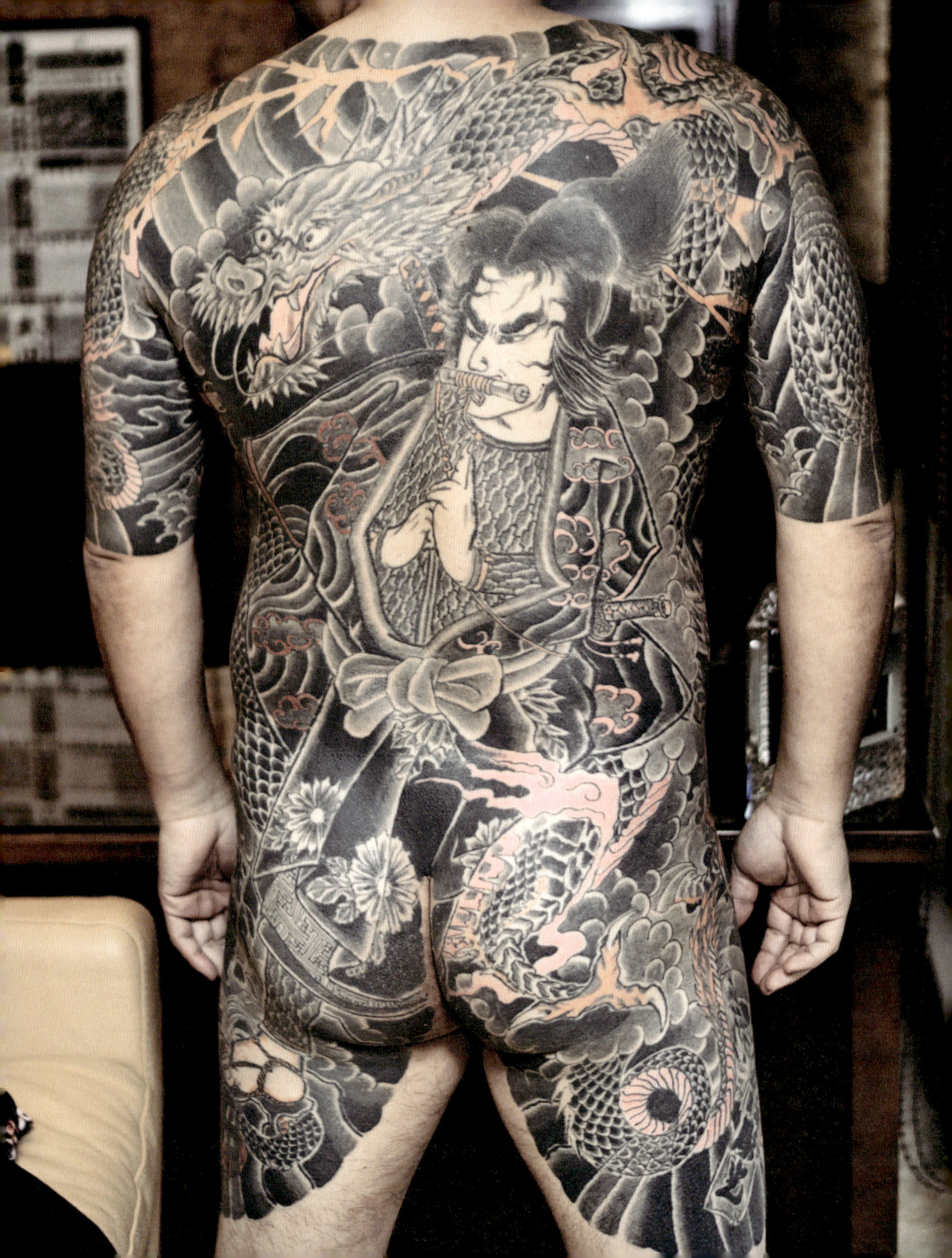

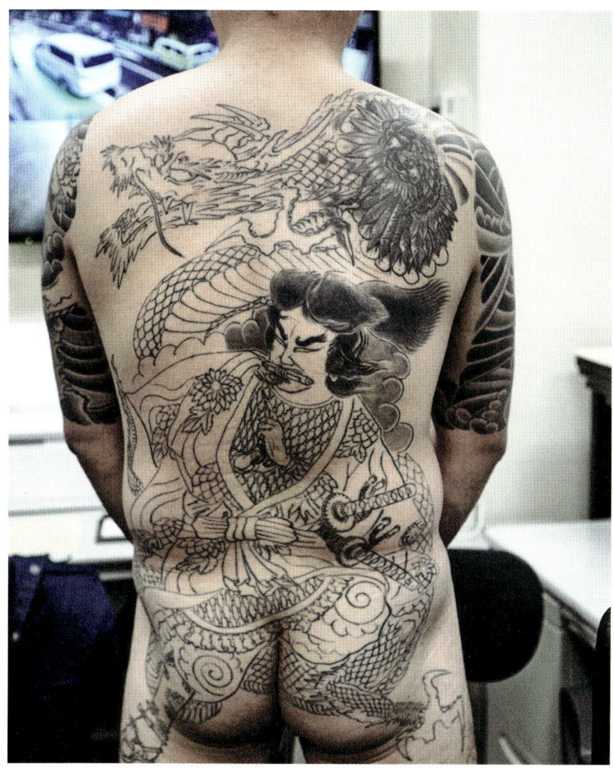

Outline of the ninja Ryuoh-Maru.

In Sweden, I bet there are old stories about Vikings and old heroes, right? It's the same in Japan. A lot of people have heard these heroic stories. They're popular because of Japanese culture – it's a nationalistic thing.

The ninja Ryuoh-Maru channelling energy.

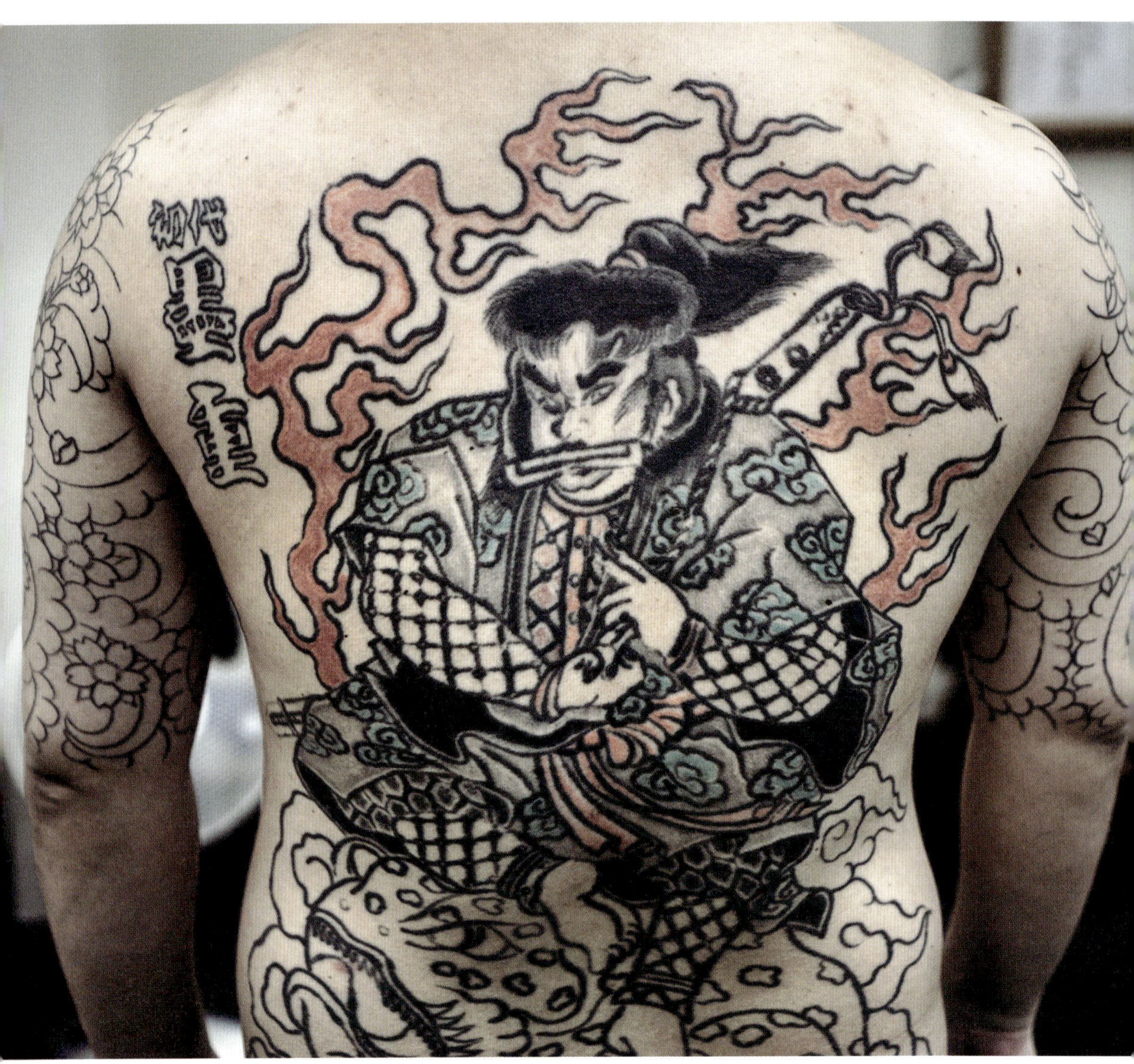

The ninja Ryuoh-Maru with thunderbolt patterns.

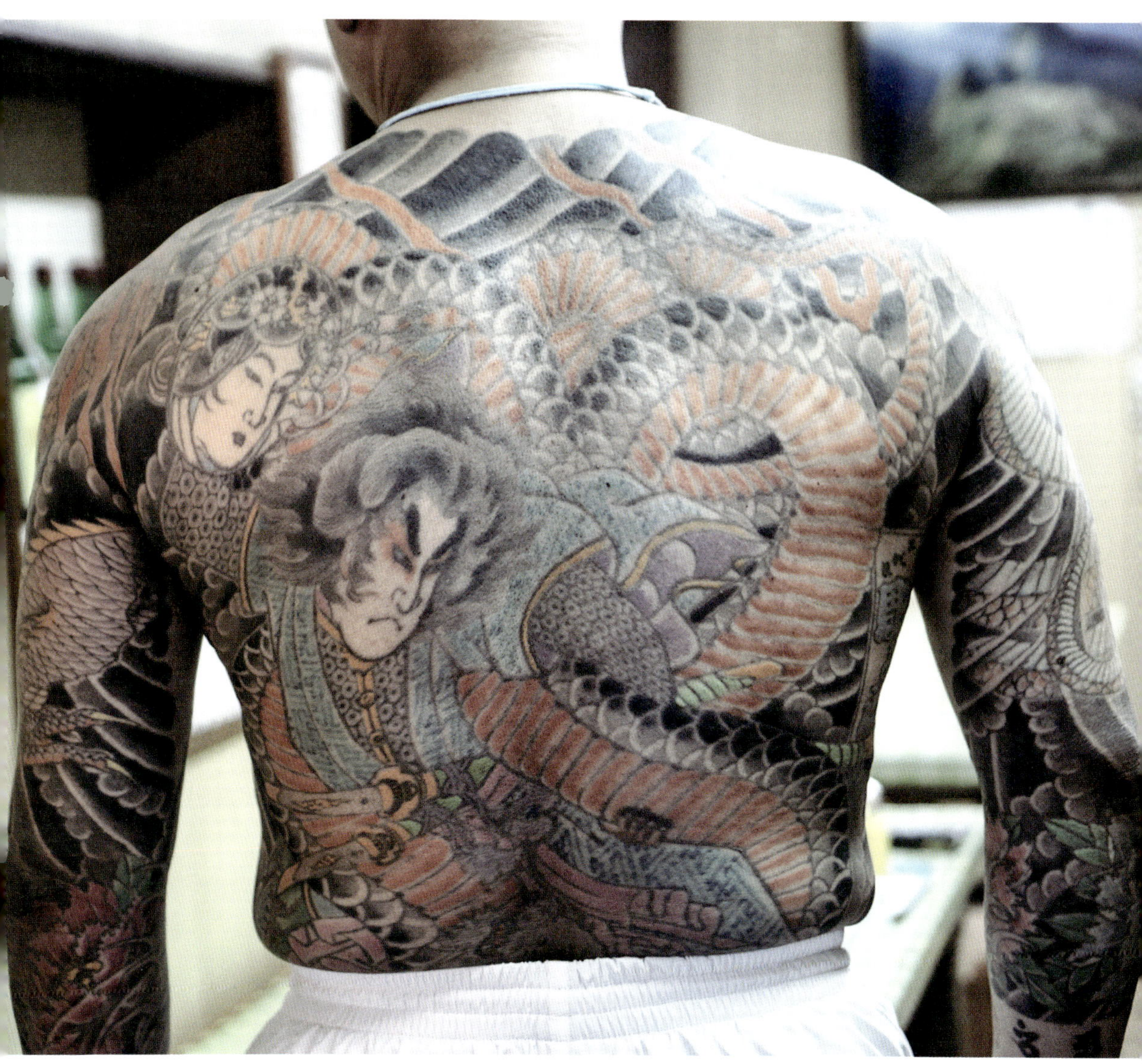

The Japanese Edo period hero Ryoutarou battling a dragon.

The Dragon & The Carp

As we have seen, yakuza members can trace the roots of their organizations back to gamblers, street peddlers and perhaps some samurai. A number of these historical concepts are illustrated on their *irezumi*. Other recurrent *irezumi* motifs include dragons and carp (koi).

The reasons given for choosing these *irezumi* is to be found in the structure of the yakuza. The most striking thing about the pyramidal structure of the organization is the *oyabun–kobun* relationship. It literary means father–child. The *oyabun* is the boss, the father, and under him he has children. This works on many levels. The *oyabun* offers protection and shelter, for example, and the child in turn pledges eternal allegiance to the boss. This loyalty to the boss has been given as one of the reasons why the yakuza has become so prominent in Japan. The system has roots that can be traced all the way back to the gambler and street peddler system mentioned above. The relationship is initiated by means of an old Shinto ritual, *sakazuki*, in which the member drinks sake with his boss from a special cup; in the particular case of my project, it is one marked with the Yamaguchi-gumi emblem. An intermediary instructs the *oyabun* to drink the sake and to leave as much as his heart tells him for the *kobun*. After the *oyabun* has drunk his sake, and the intermediate has refilled the cup, the *kobun* finishes the sake and puts away the empty cup in his kimono.

It is the *oyabun-kobun* structure the yakuza speak of when they talk about the dragon and the carp. The dragon, in a sense, represents the boss, or the desire to become a boss. The dragon has a long history as a symbol in Japan. Today, it encompasses Chinese, Indian and indigenous narratives such as folk tales. In one of the earliest interpretations, it represents a water god. According to Buddhist legend, dragons rule over the ocenas and rivers. But they are not only associated with water; they can also be spotted on mountains and in valleys. Numerous historical texts belonging to a variety of genres discuss their color and number of legs. Dragons also share features with other animals such as the scales of a carp or the horns of a deer. Dragons thus have a rich and diverse history. The yakuzas' explanations show that the reason for getting a dragon *irezumi* differs from person to person. The one thing that the yakuzas' descriptions of dragons have in common is that they are powerful.

Carp, like dragons, are mentioned as symbols of a desire to climb the hierarchical ladder of the organization. Carp, depicted in myth as swimming upstream and eventually turning into a dragon, represent endurance and courage. Another story that involves a carp, and which appears frequently in the motifs of Japanese *irezumi* is the one about Kintaro (golden boy), a well-known figure in traditional folklore. There are also several stories about another famous hero battling a giant fish. The yakuza I talked to were inspired by stories about how the carp struggles to become a dragon.

The yakuza structure is complex, and there are different structures for different syndicates. We will, however, stick to the example of the Yamaguchi-gumi. My key interview subject, Ken-San, is the boss of a third-level organization within the Yamaguchi-gumi syndicate. At the same time, he is also ranked number four in the second-level organization, the Masuda-gumi, which is also part of the Yamaguchi-gumi. The whole structure thus resembles a pyramid. At the top of Yamaguchi-gumi is a godfather, and he has direct subordinates who in turn have their own subordinates. This is the chain of command.

Another symbol that sometimes appears on yakuza tattoos is also connected to the organizational structure. Each clan is recognized by a symbol. The clan symbol is less visible these days, but it is occasionally used as a motif. The Yamaguchi-gumi symbol is diamond-shaped and made up of the characters *yama* and *guchi* (山口). Sometimes it includes the family name. The pins and stickers I was shown featured the name Masuda. It means that the Masuda family (*gumi*) is part of the Yamaguchi-gumi clan. The pins differ according to rank. The highest-ranking members wear platinum pins, and prominent members of second-rank families wear gold pins. Members of the Yamaguchi-gumi even used to have business cards with their names and symbols. These cannot be used anymore because of new, stricter laws against the yakuza. The altered appearance of the yakuza is due to the same reason. Even though it seems that the yakuza is going underground, the symbol is sometimes present in their *irezumi*, but in the cases that I have seen, only the diamond is tattooed.

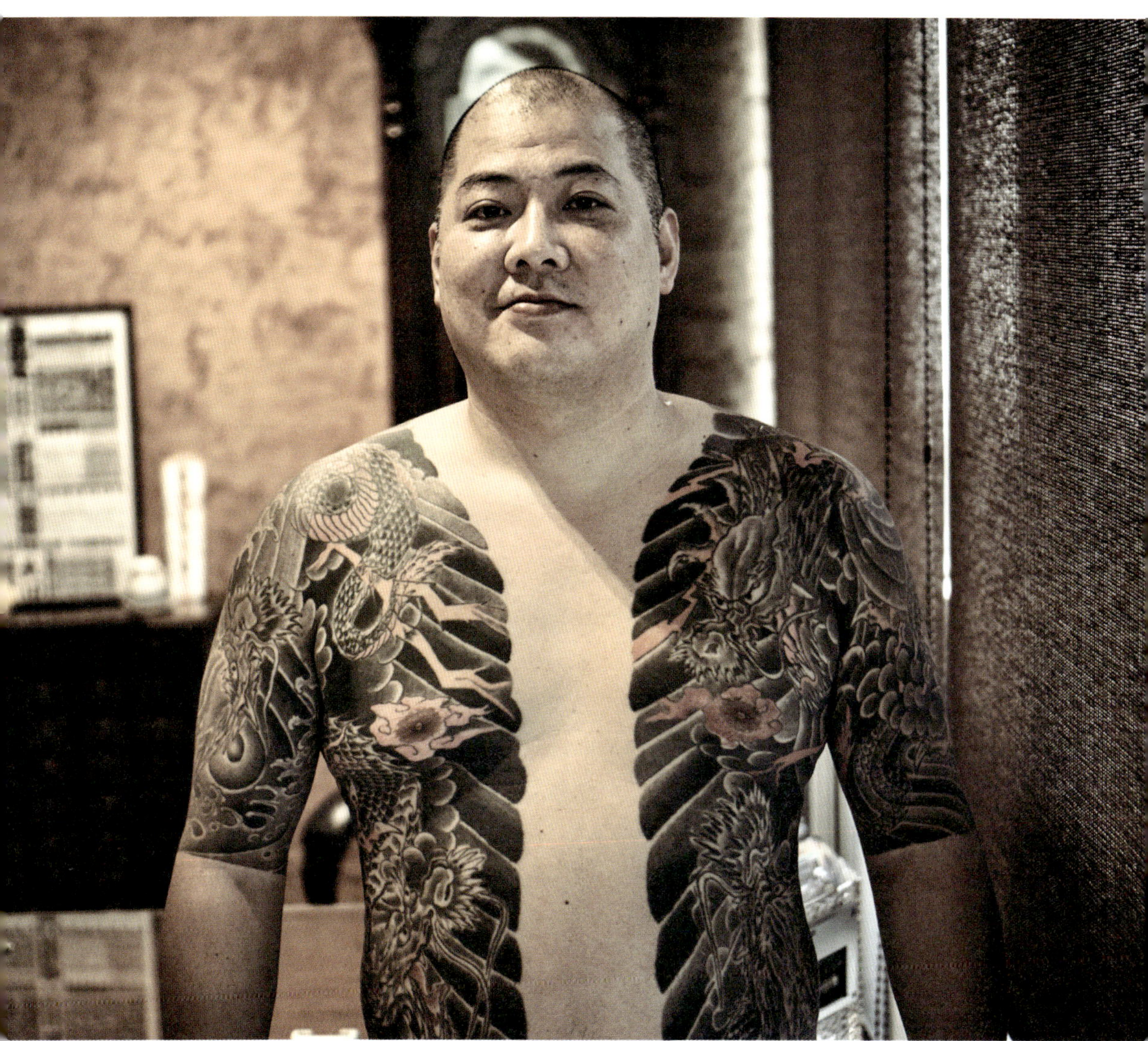
Four dragons and thunderbolt patterns on a traditional Japanese suit *irezumi*.

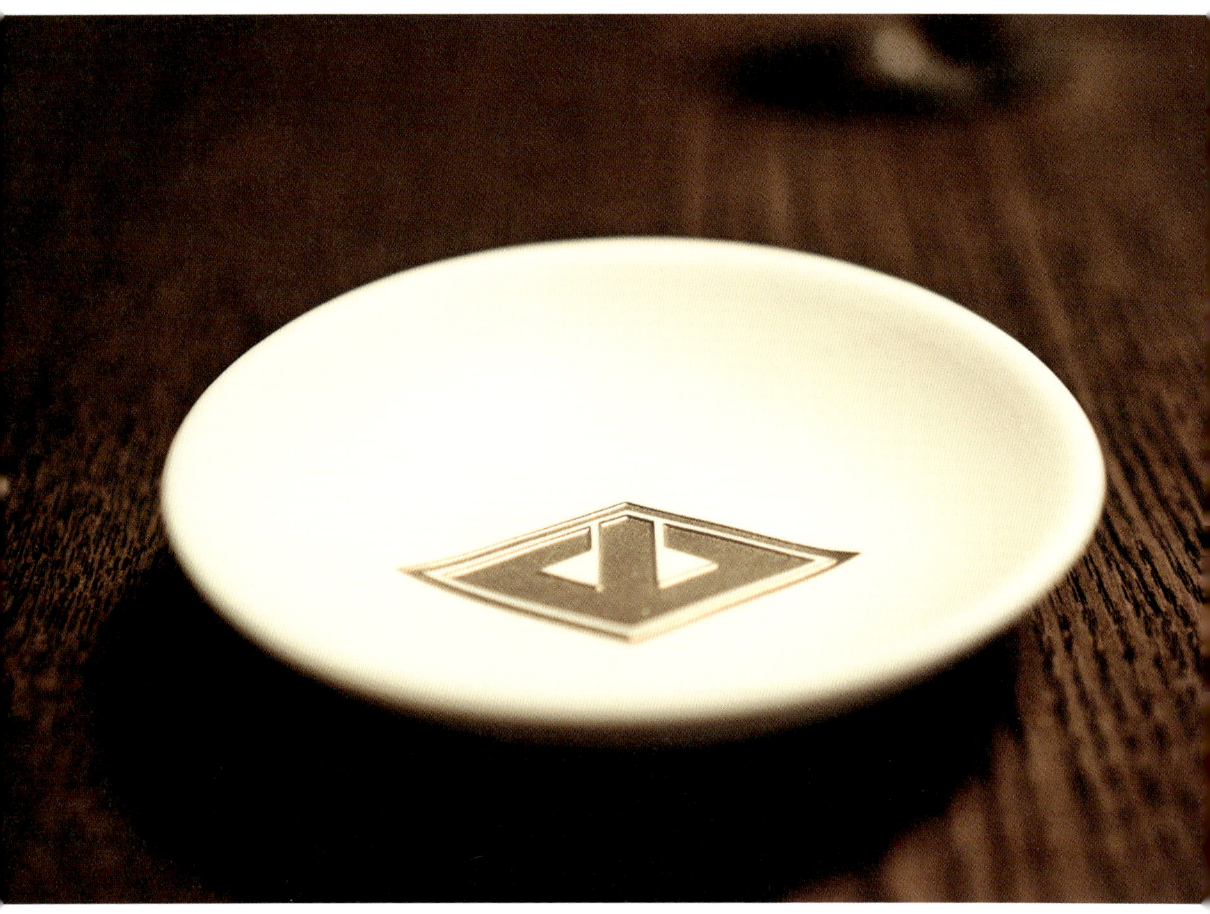

Sakazuki cup with the Yamaguchi-gumi symbol (yamabishi, diamond). It is used in rituals that are performed when a new member joins a yakuza family.

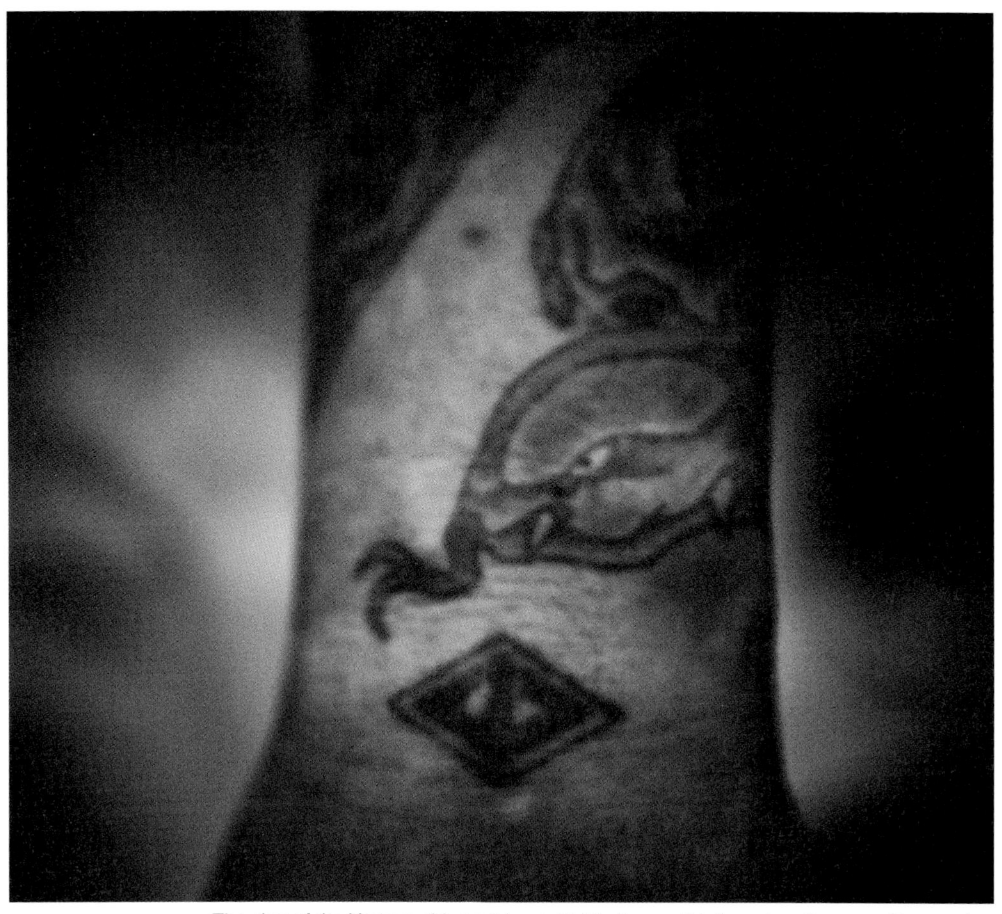

The sign of the Yamaguchi-gumi (yamabishi, diamond) tattooed on the arm with a snake.

When I was a young teenager, I didn't study; I just kept getting into fights. And before I knew it, I was in a [yakuza] family. I was never really interested in joining, but growing up doing all this bad stuff, I decided to join. It was my best opportunity; I couldn't stop doing bad things.

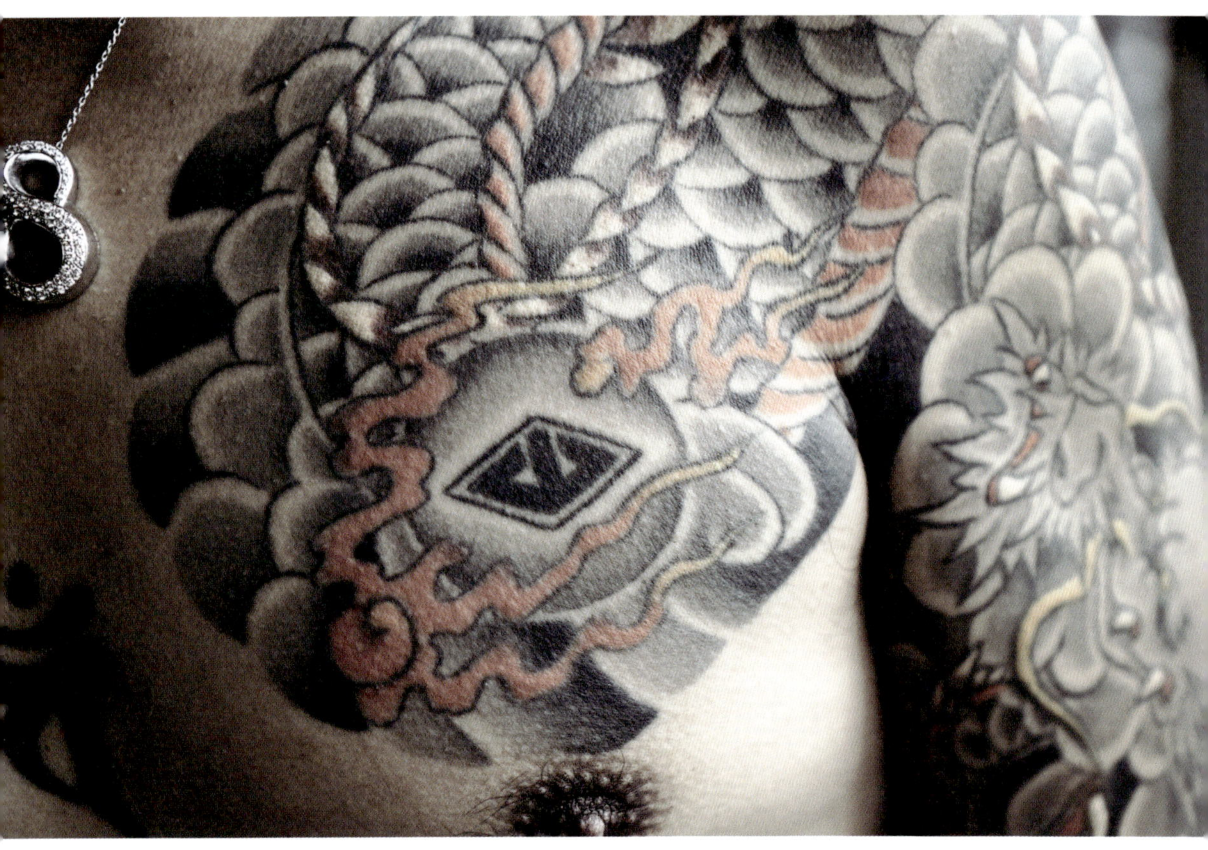

The Yamaguchi-gumi symbol (yamabishi, diamond) tattooed on the chest.

I've been a yakuza all my life, and I'll be a yakuza until my last breath. I don't know what it's like to live a normal life. I got the Yamaguchi-gumi diamond to remind me that this is forever. Even if my life is taken, I will still wear it.

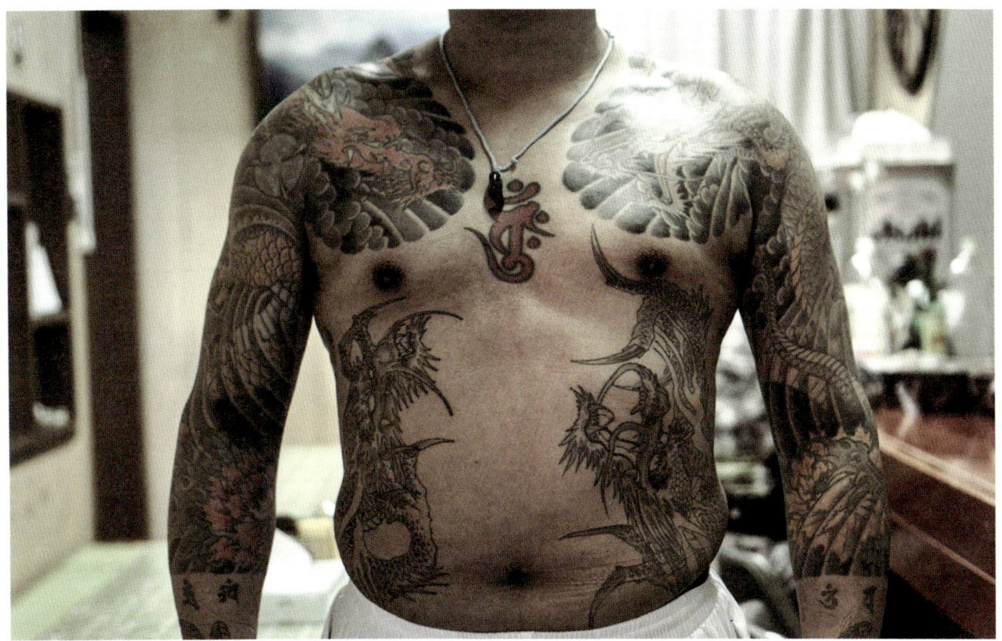

Four dragons in a symmetrical pattern on the chest and abdomen.

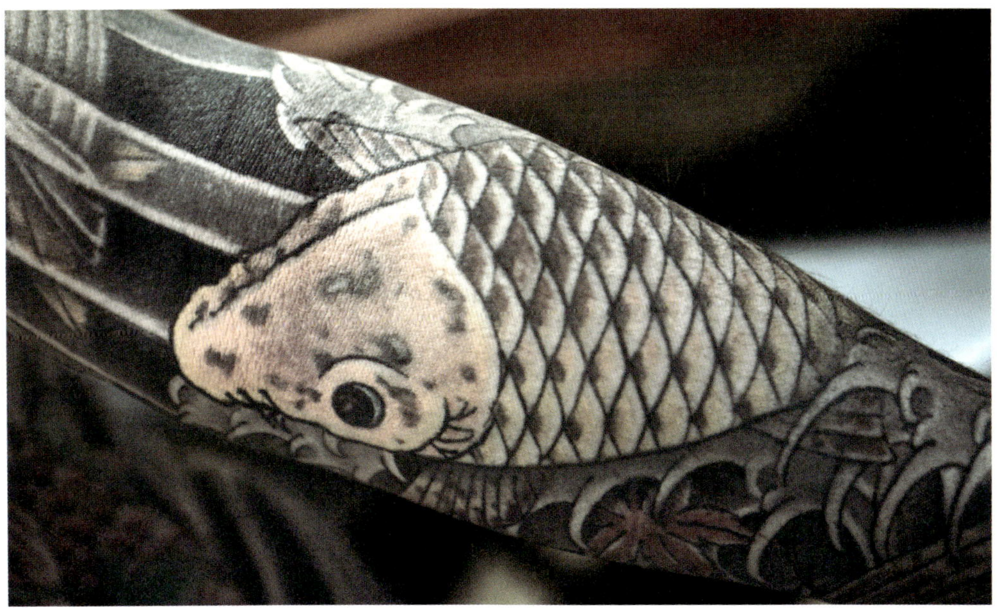

Close-up of koi fish.

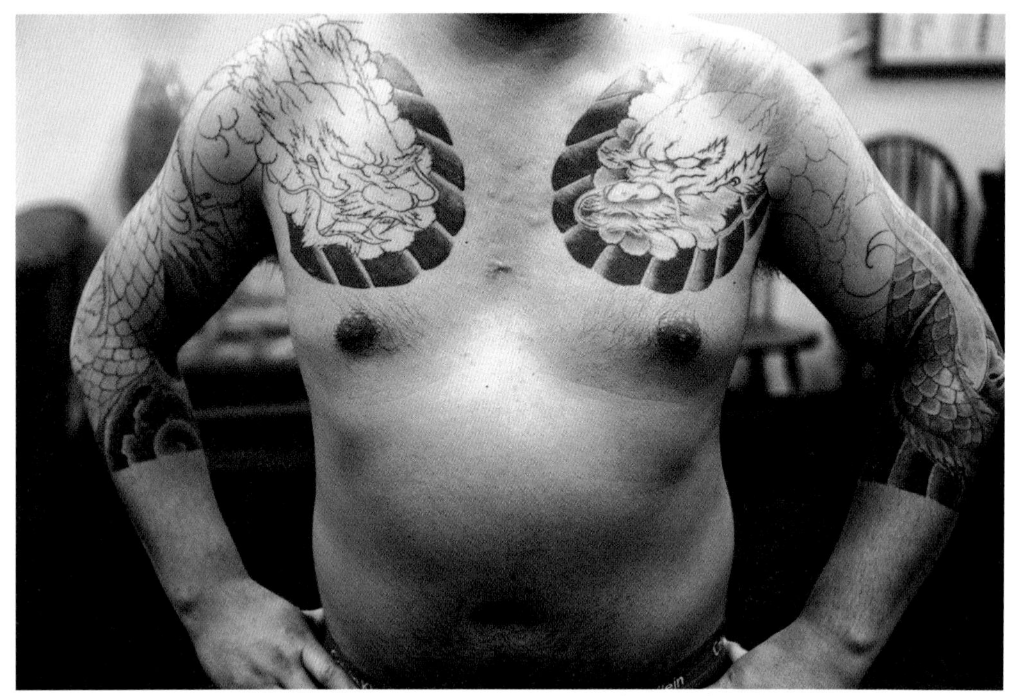

Outlines of two dragons on a young yakuza.

Everyone is getting the carp irezumi because they want to move forward and become a dragon. But I want to be a dragon as quickly as I can. That's why I chose the dragon irezumi. I want to be number one.

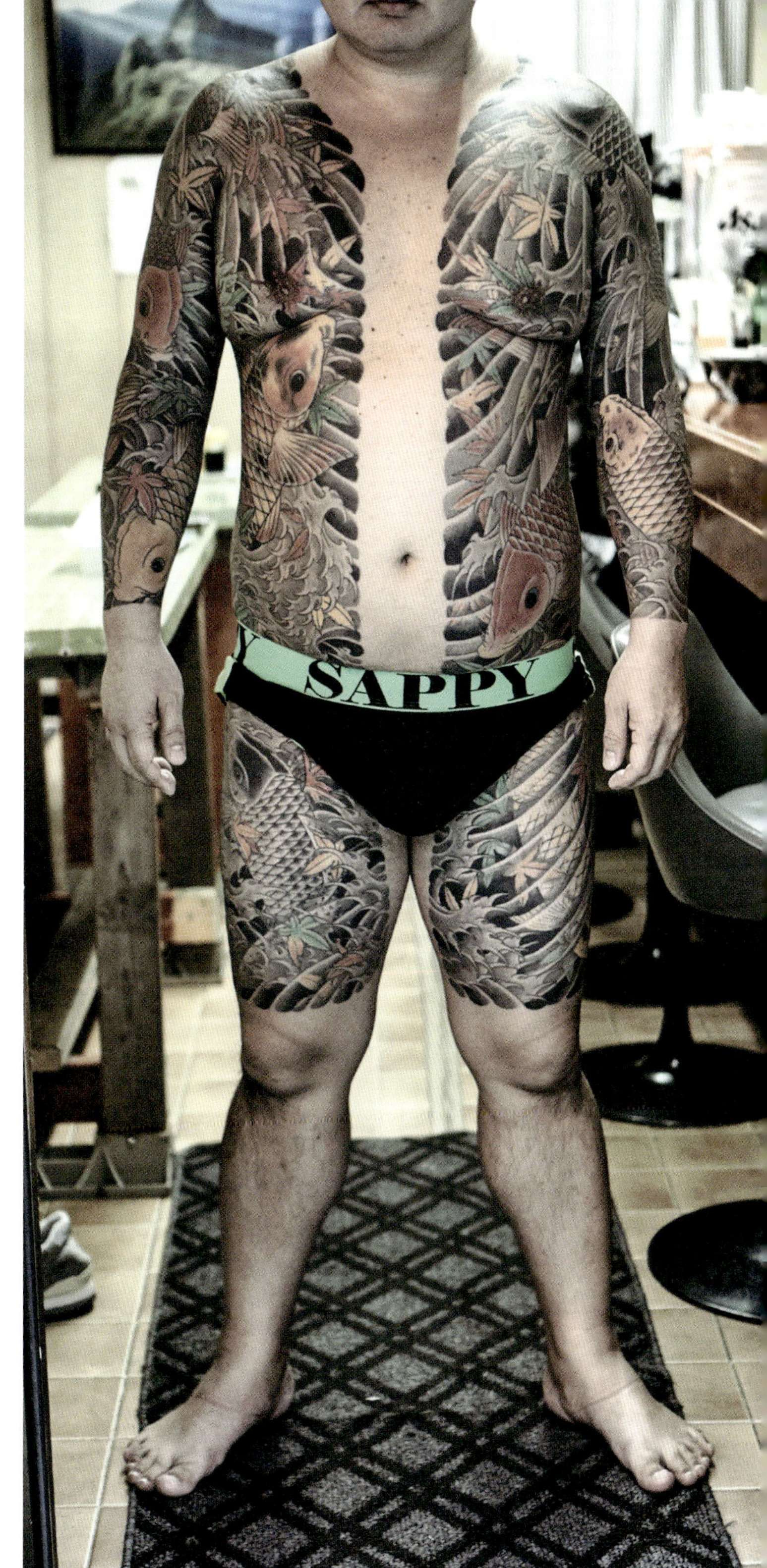

Fish and leaves. A traditional, symmetrical suit *irezumi* pattern.

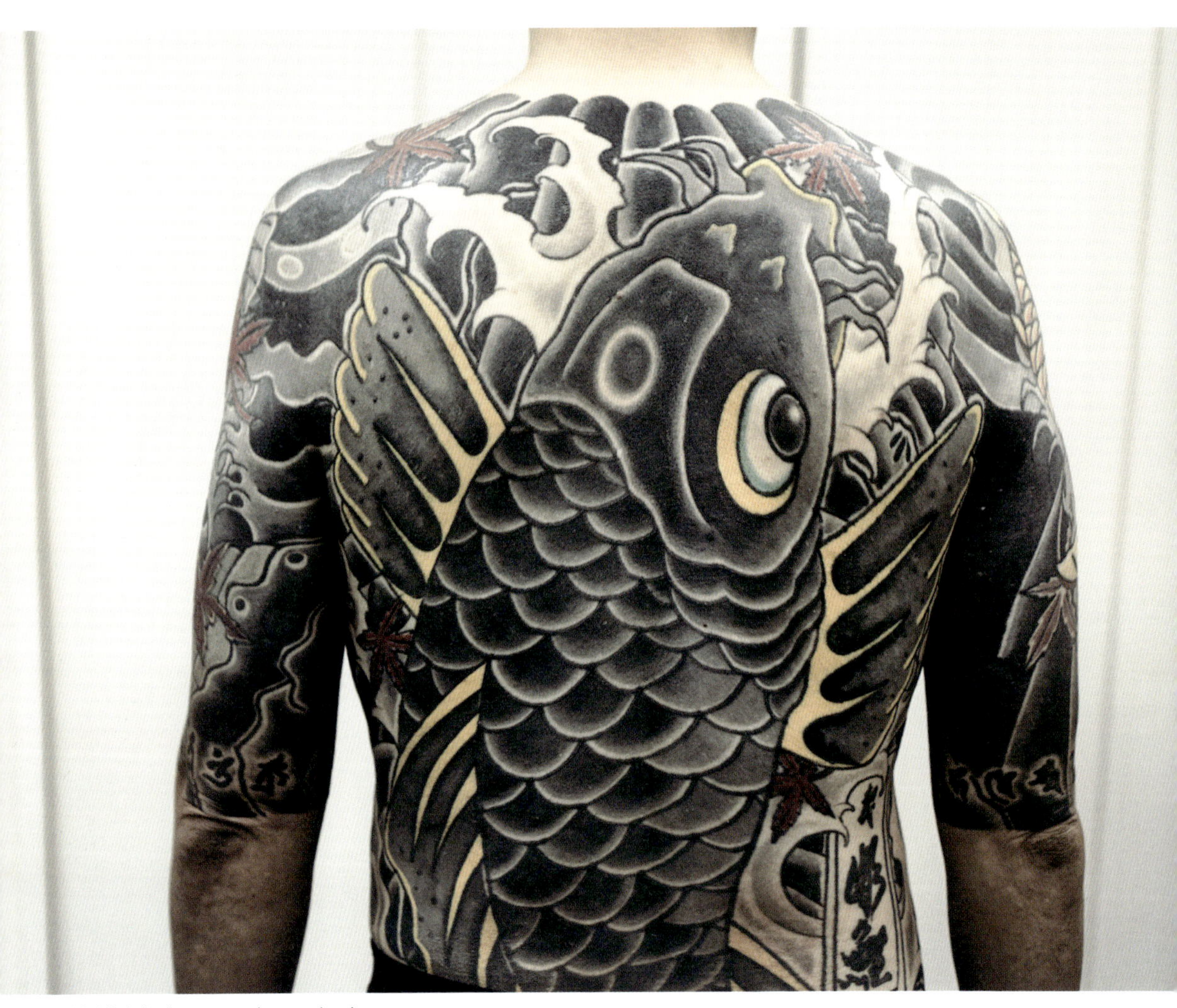

Koi fish facing upwards on a back.

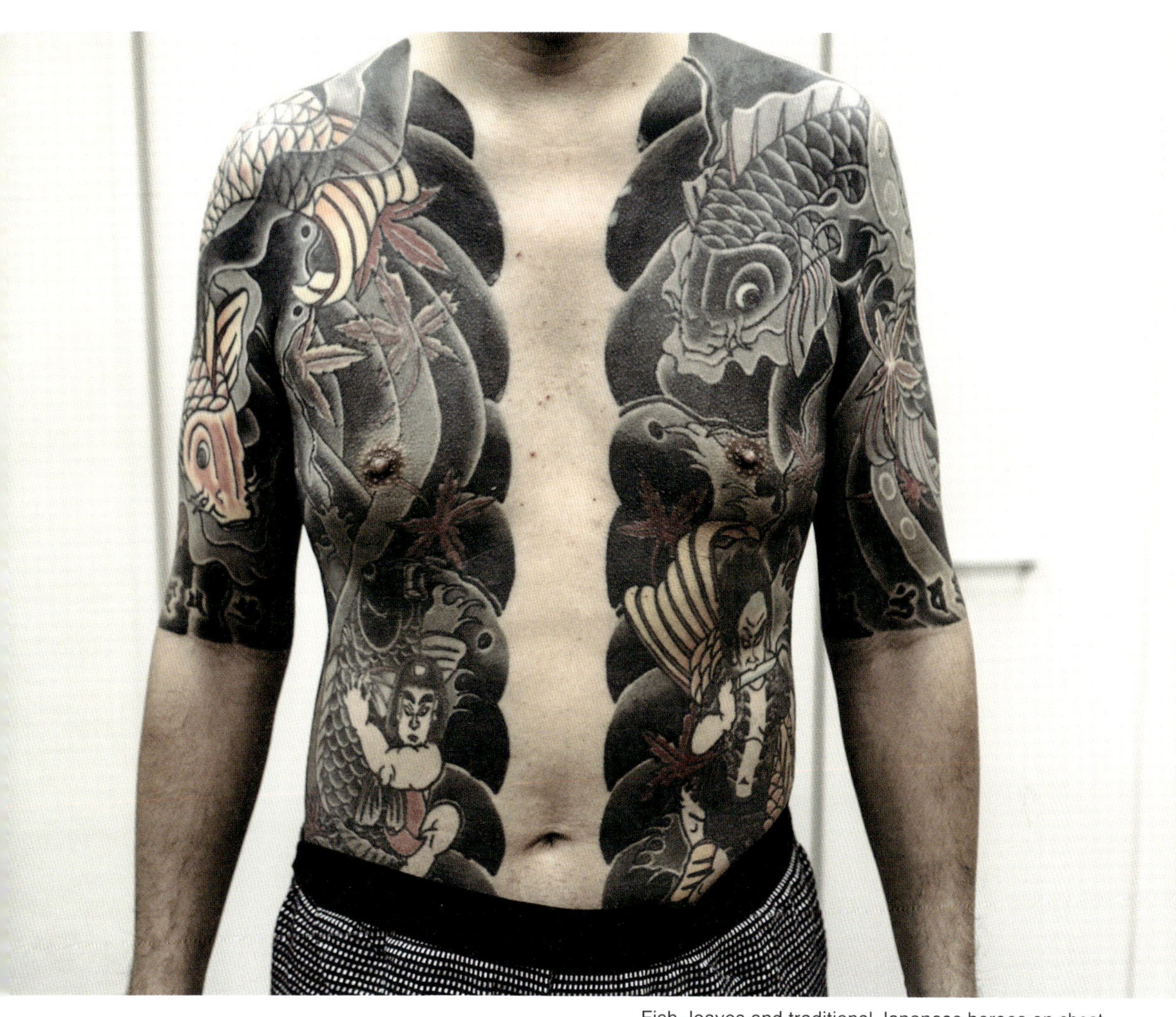

Fish, leaves and traditional Japanese heroes on chest.

The dragon is considered to be a really strong image. I got the dragon on the front since I already had an irezumi on my back. The dragon is power-ful, good. Like the old Vikings had a dragon at the front of their ships. The meaning can be the same as that.

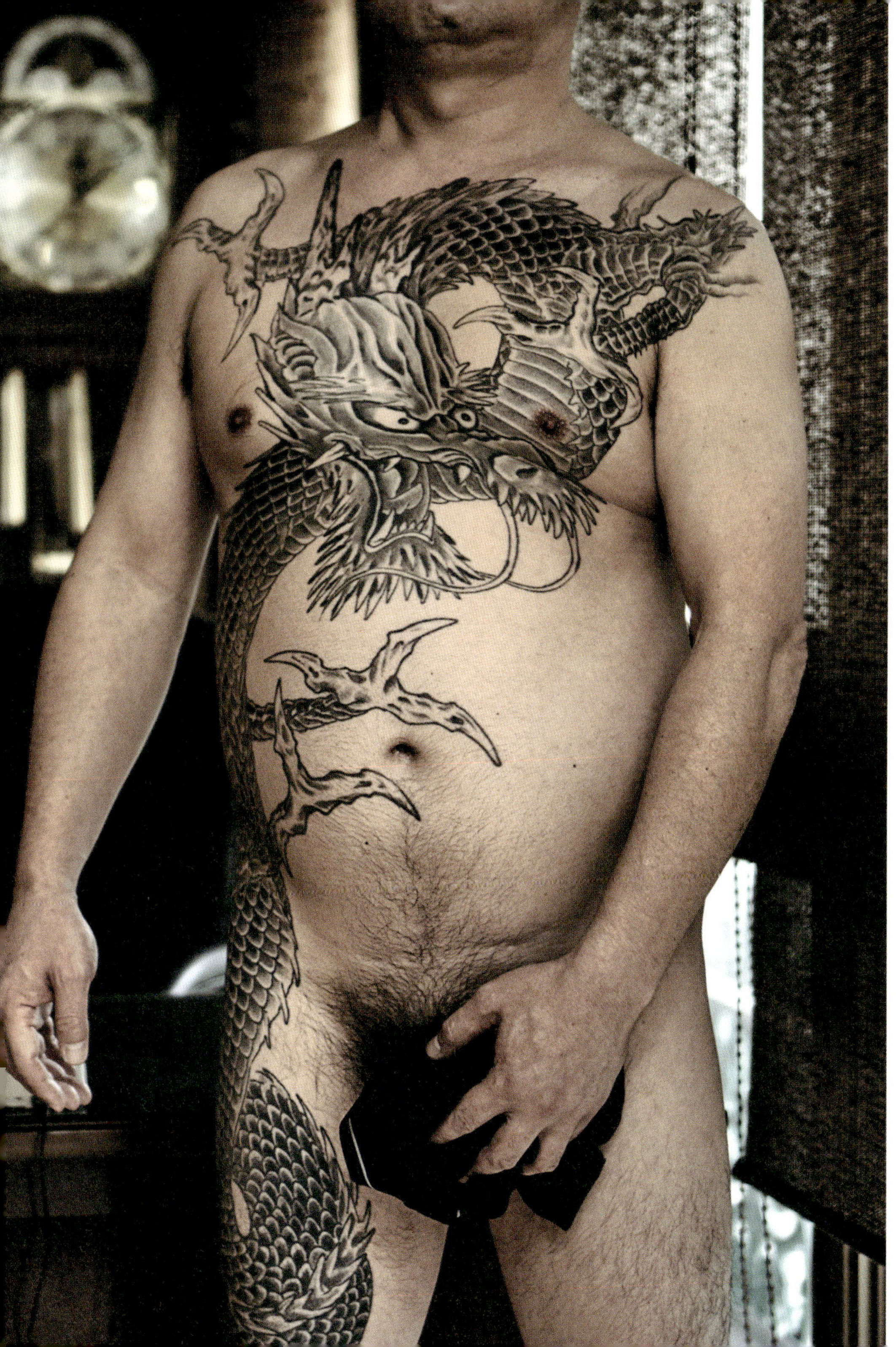

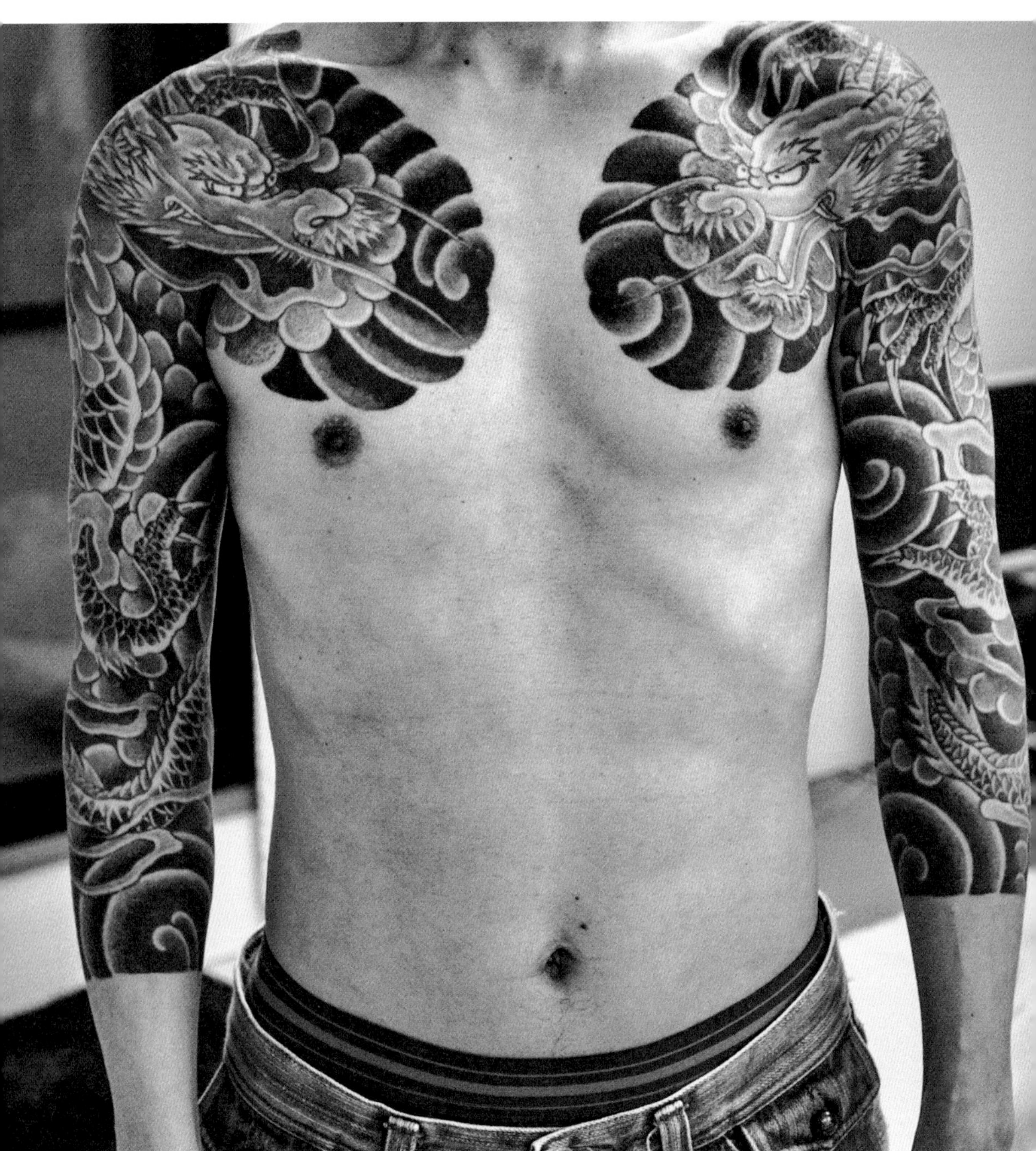

Two dragon *irezumi* on chest and arms.

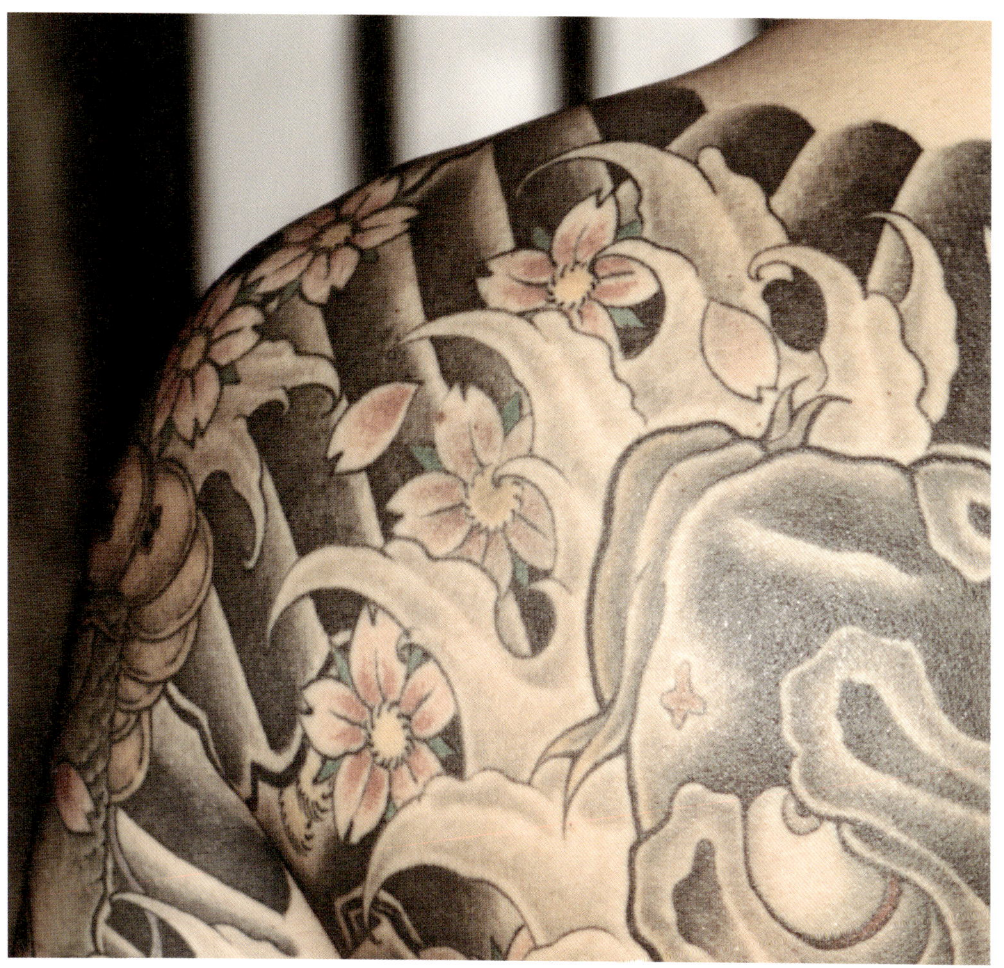

Irezumi with decorative cherry blossoms.

Before you drink the sakazuki with your boss, there are a lot of things you need to do. I still remember that day. It was an important day for me. It was six years ago. You drink it step by step. If you're moving upwards in the pyramid, you drink with the boss above you. When I drank it, I felt a sense of responsibility. I felt that I needed to become more active and get stronger.

Grey dragon *irezumi* on chest.

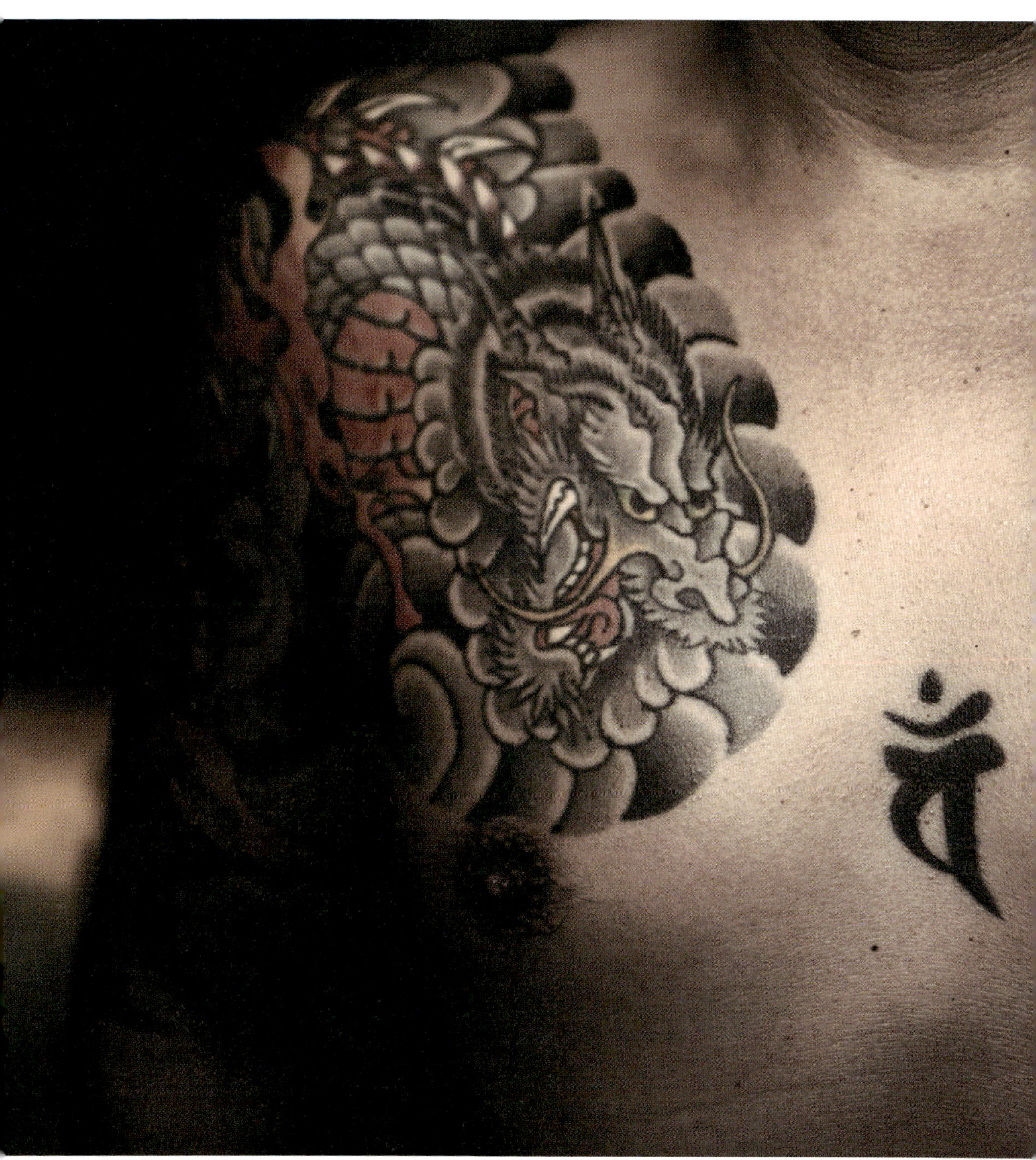

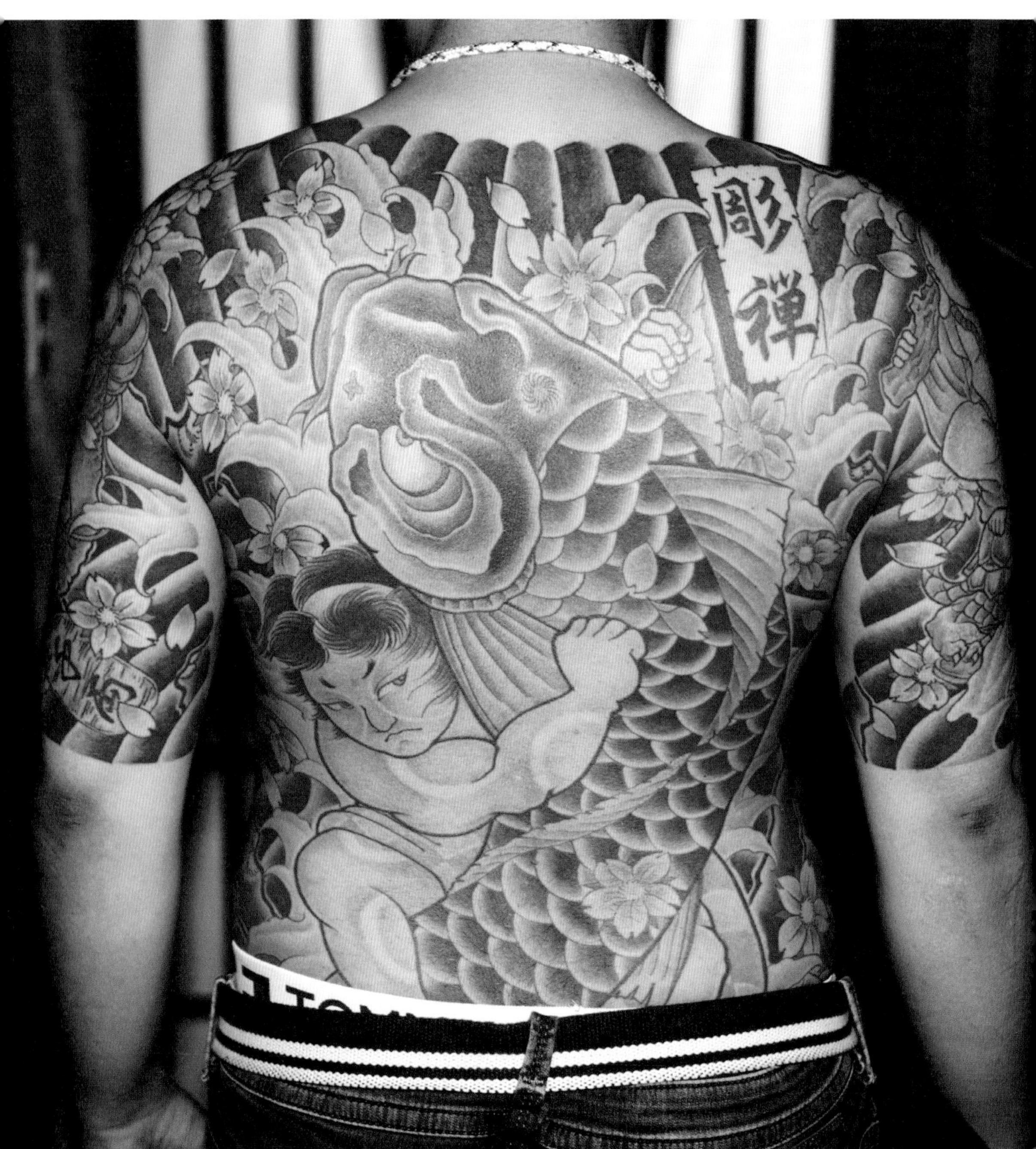

The koi on my back is facing upwards. It's trying to get to the top, just like me. In Japan, the carp goes up the river and becomes a dragon. That's the story. It means that I'm always heading upwards.

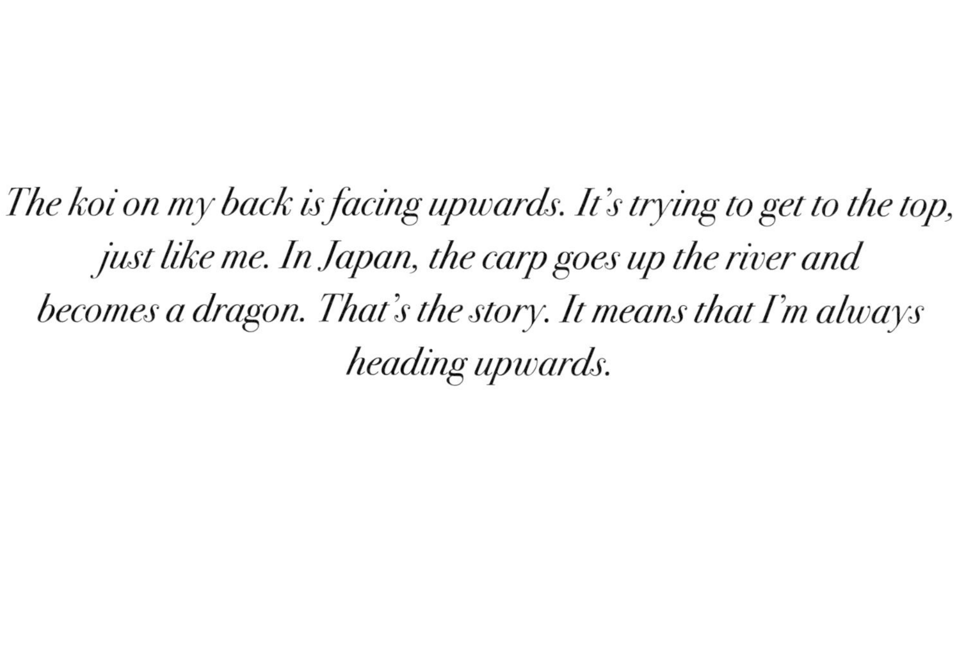

Koi fish and the story of the Kintaor *irezumi*.

Gods & Spirits

There are many Buddhist symbols on Japanese *irezumi*. One of them is Fudo Myoo (Acala), often portrayed with a sword and surrounded by fire. He often appears in the form of a demon, which is misleading. He is the protector of Buddhism and known for having been a wise king. Many images and statues of Fudo Myoo are found throughout Japan. Even though Fudo Myoo is not a demon, these are found on Japanese *irezumi*. Originating in stories about the Buddhist idea of hell, they are thought to be powerful beings.

The seven gods of fortune is another popular image. Sometimes only one of these gods is tattooed. A yakuza who had an *irezumi* of Hotei told me that he chose this motif because he wanted protection for both his inner and outer wealth. One goddess that is commonly tattooed is the bodhisattva Kannon, the goddess of mercy. She is regularly pictured with a halo around her head and a dragon. Sometimes the classical stories of the gods that are chosen for an *irezumi* are adapted to suit the person wearing the tattoo. Just as the spirits and gods possess power, it was explained to me that different animals also have powers that can offer protection for the individuals that have them tattooed on their bodies.

In response to the question of which *irezumi* motifs to avoid, the boss made it clear to me that certain symbols that younger yakuza might select would not be good for them.

"Putting a skull on your body, or a chopped-off head. They get it from old Japanese art. These you should not get without understanding the meaning of the design. It's bad luck, but people still do it. It's a bad omen. If you get a tattoo of a lady, you'll have trouble with a lot of ladies because you make the ladies jealous."

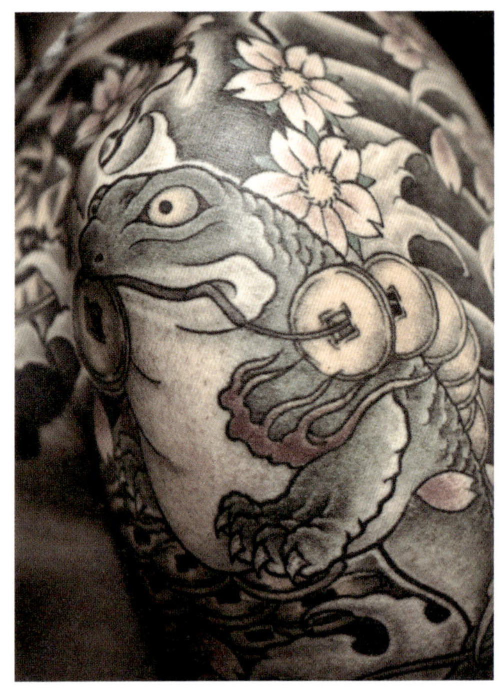

The kairu, or frog, for good luck.

The frog: Kairu, it means that no matter where you go, you'll always come back. So, if I spend a lot of money, that money will come home. I also have one of the seven gods; it means the same as the frog. When I was growing up, we were quite poor. That's why I chose to do the money – because I want to become rich. You know, we had food on the table, but it was nothing fancy. It was poor man's food. And the dragon is there to protect the money.

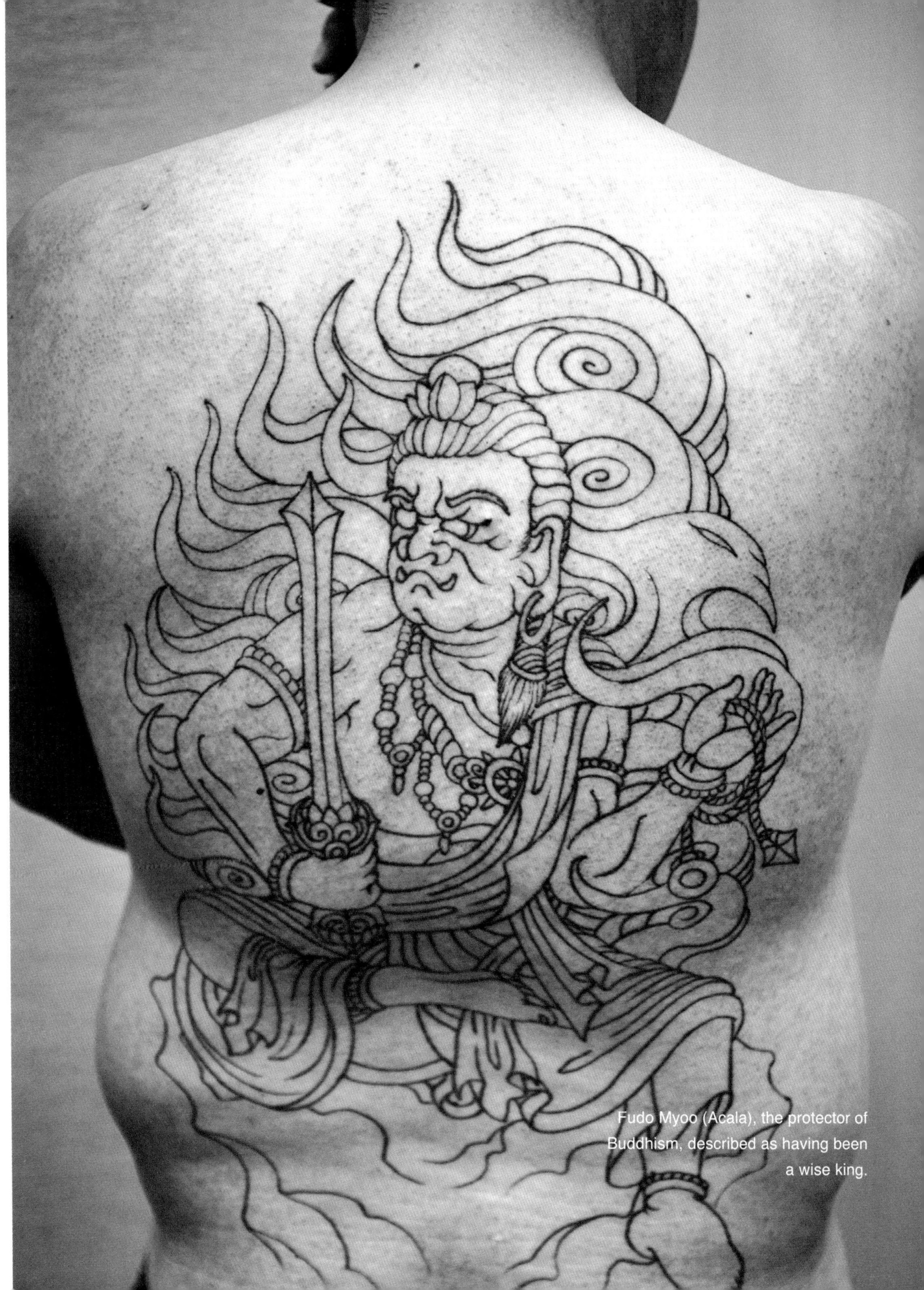

Fudo Myoo (Acala), the protector of
Buddhism, described as having been
a wise king.

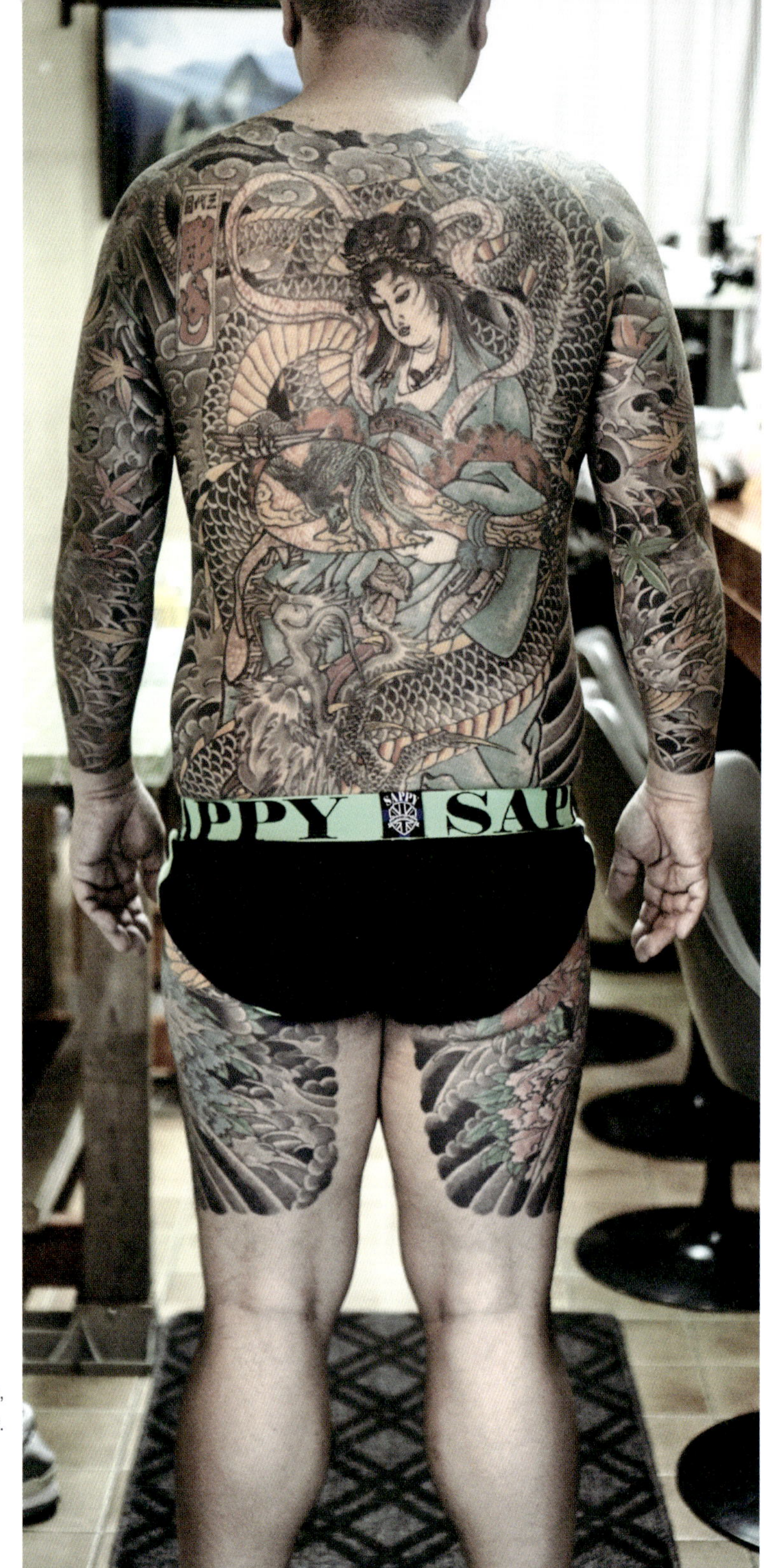

Bodhisattva Kannon,
the goddess of mercy.

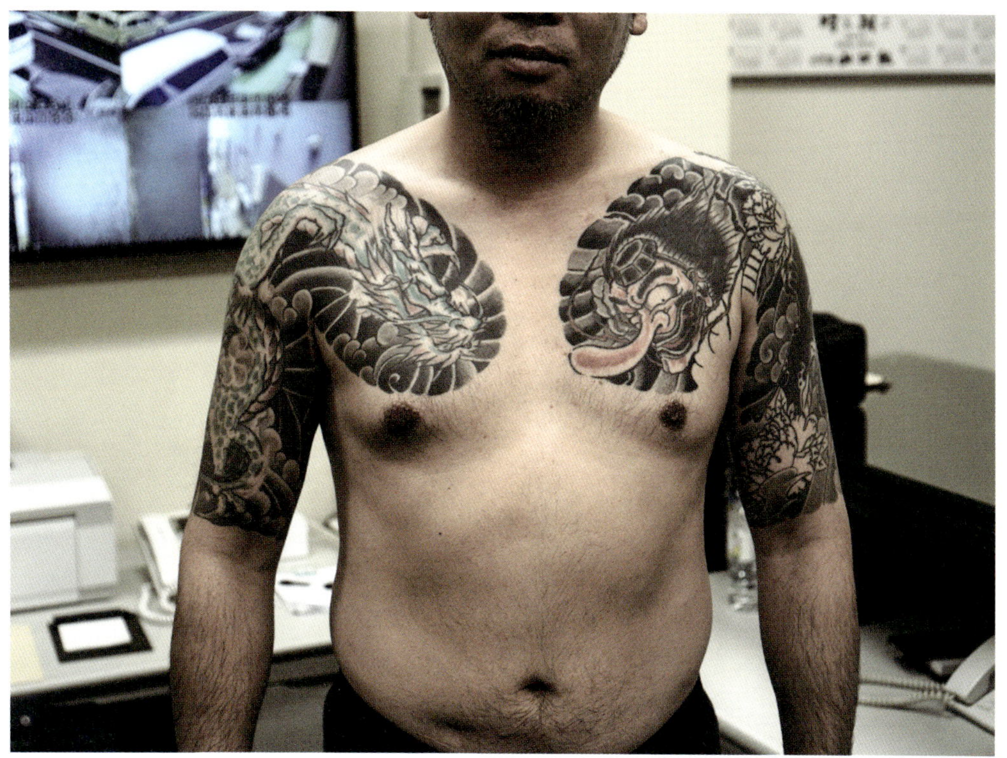

Green dragon and tengu mask.

*Many yakuza have their own opinions about their irezumi,
so I decided to go with this one. I chose this irezumi
because it symbolizes me, and it's a very powerful irezumi.
This is Tengu, a Japanese god.*

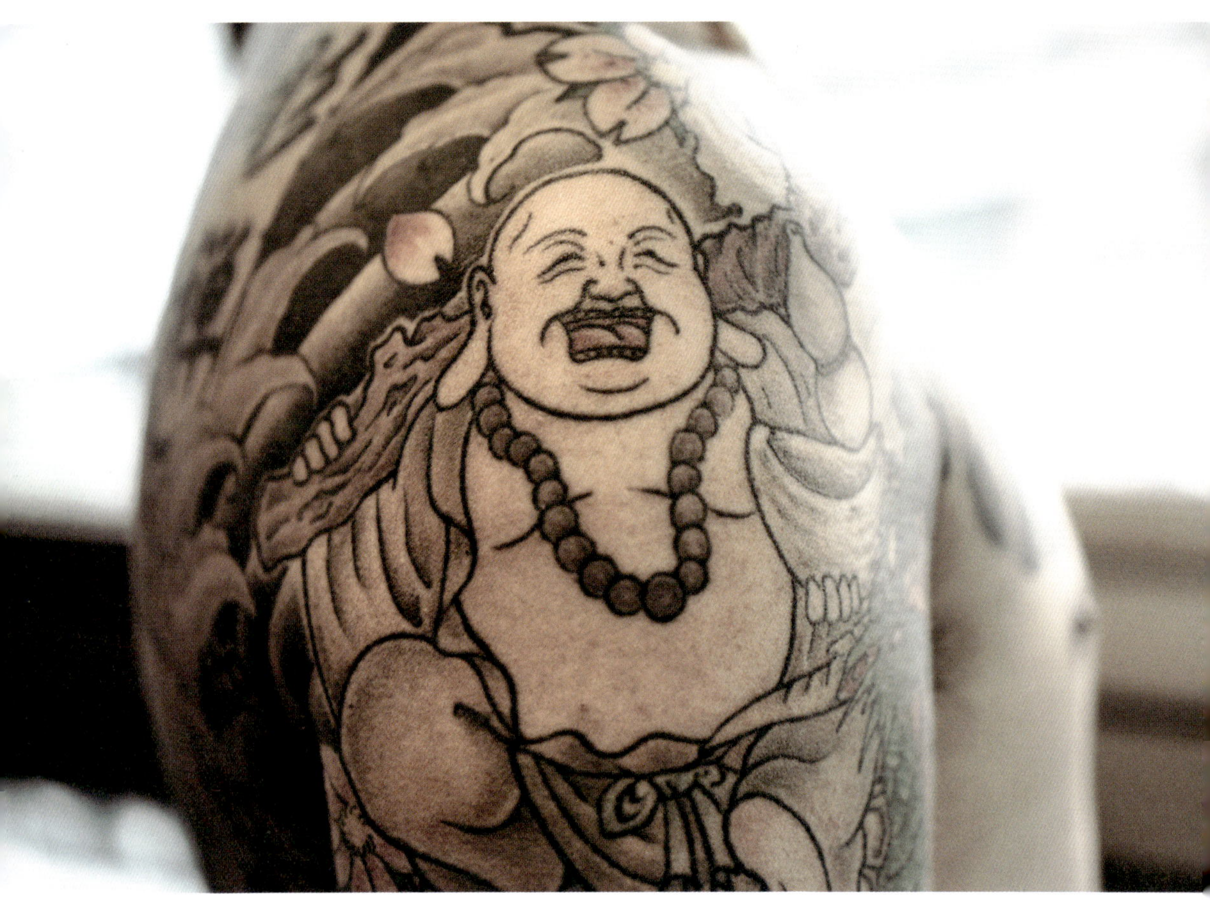

Hotei, one of the seven gods of fortune.

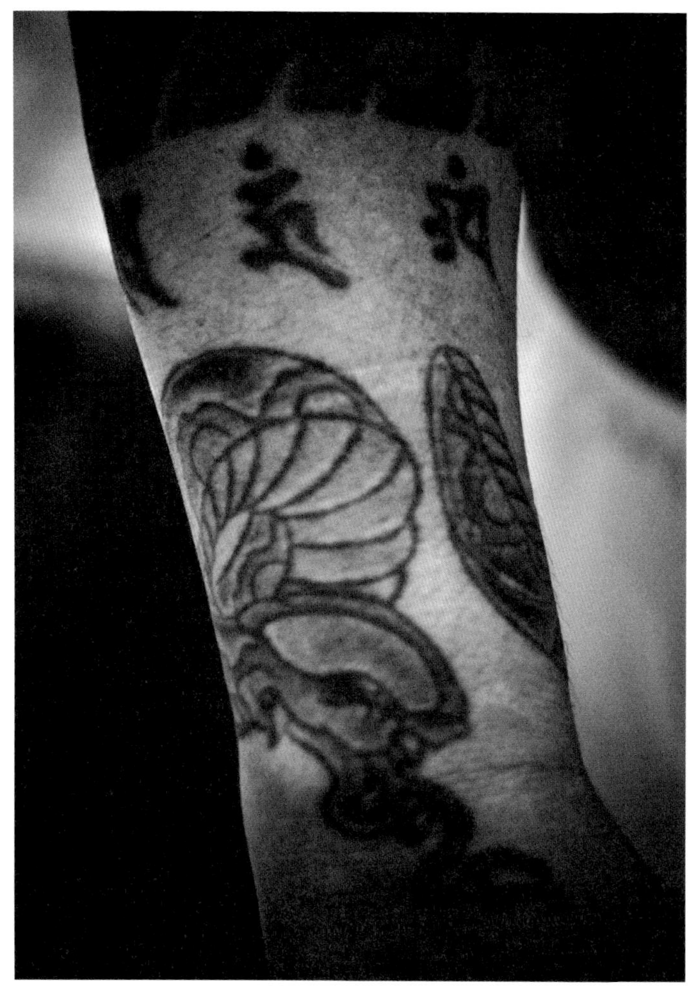

A snake on the arm of a yakuza.

I tattooed the snake because I didn't want to draw any bad spirits to me. It protects me from harm and bad spirits.

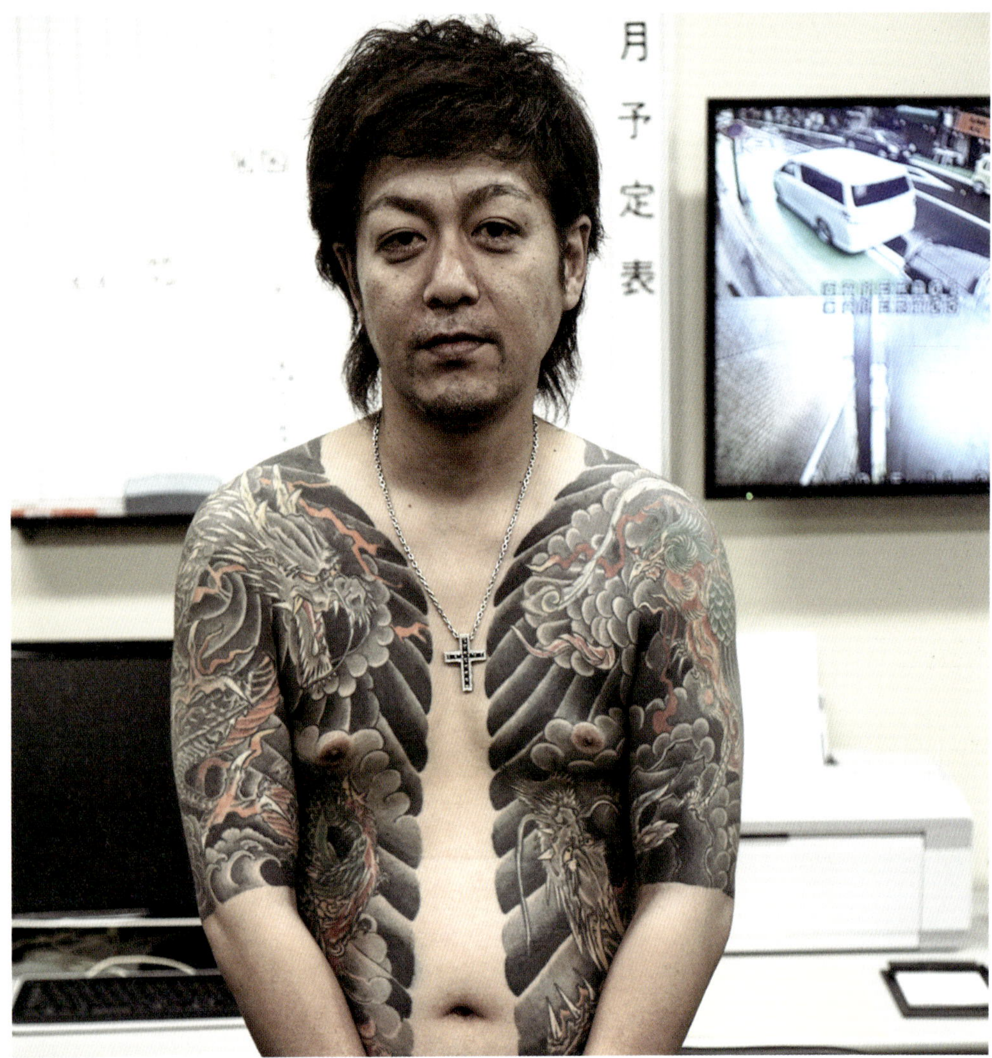

A grey dragon and a phoenix on the chest.

I chose the phoenix, since it always wins. It never dies.
It always rises again. It suits me.

Bodhisattva Kannon, the goddess of mercy.

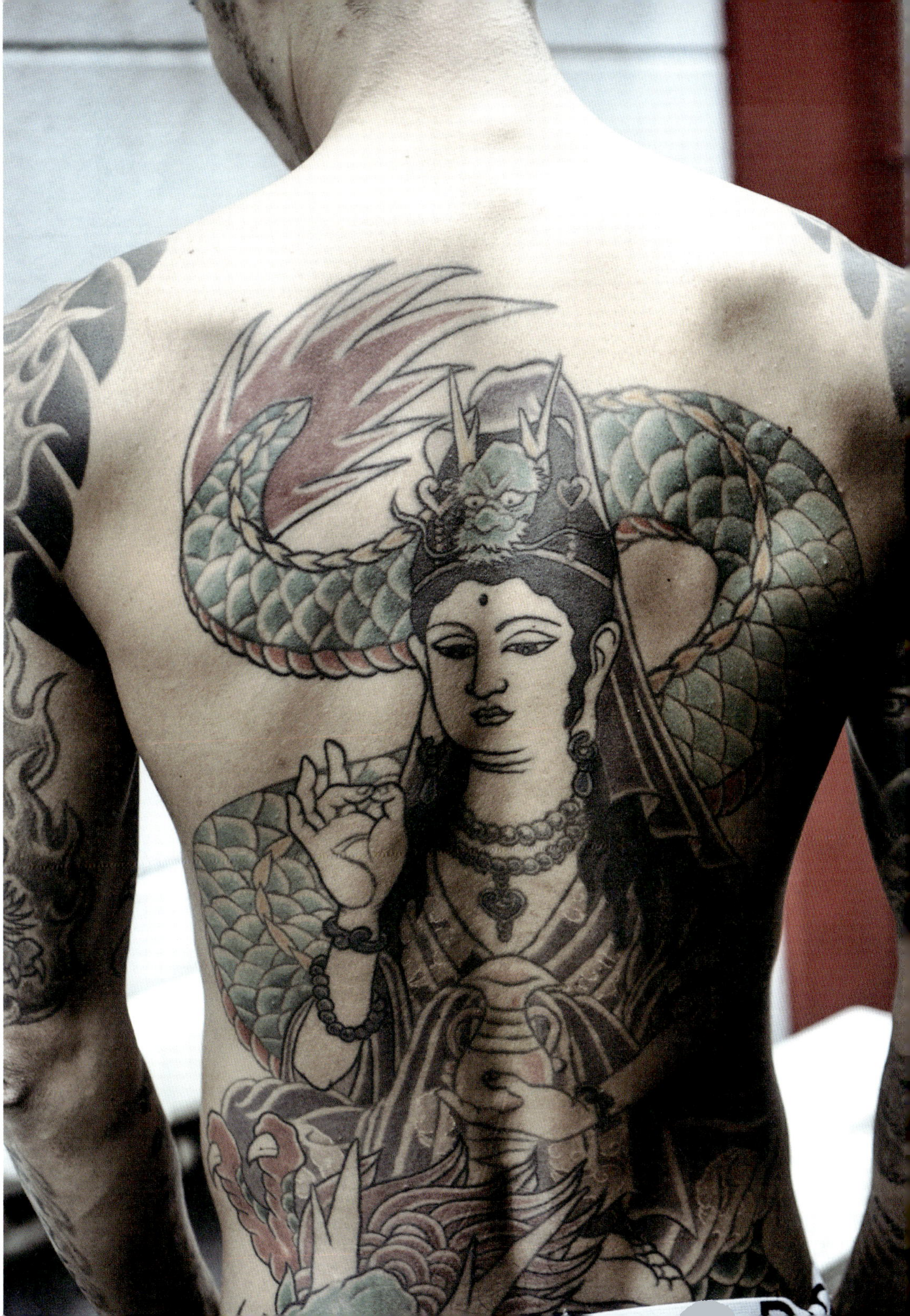

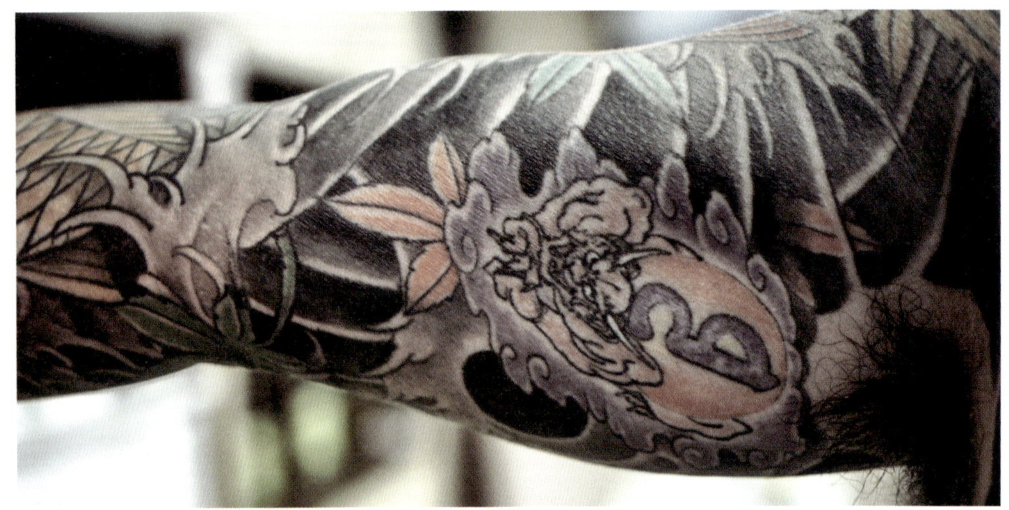

A purple *'oni* demon holding a zodiac sign.

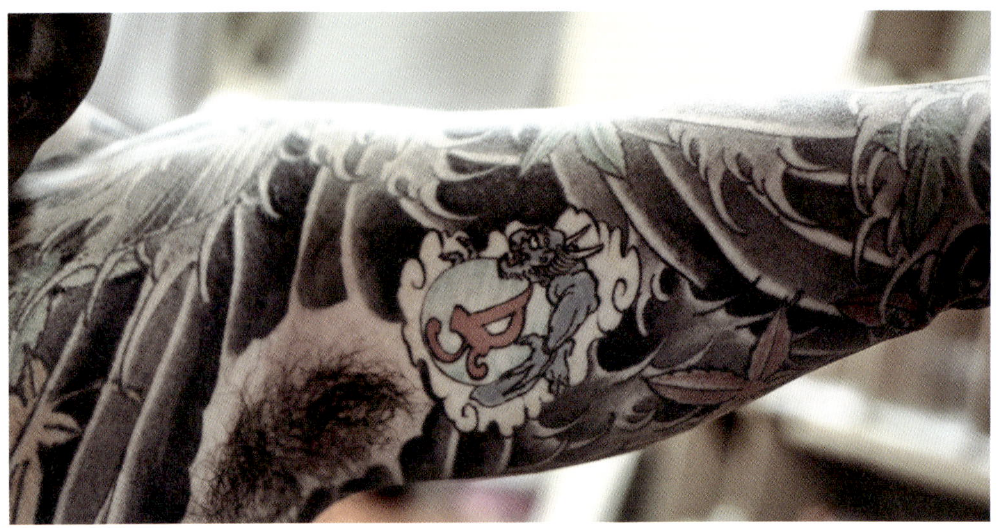

A blue *'oni* demon holding a zodiac sign.

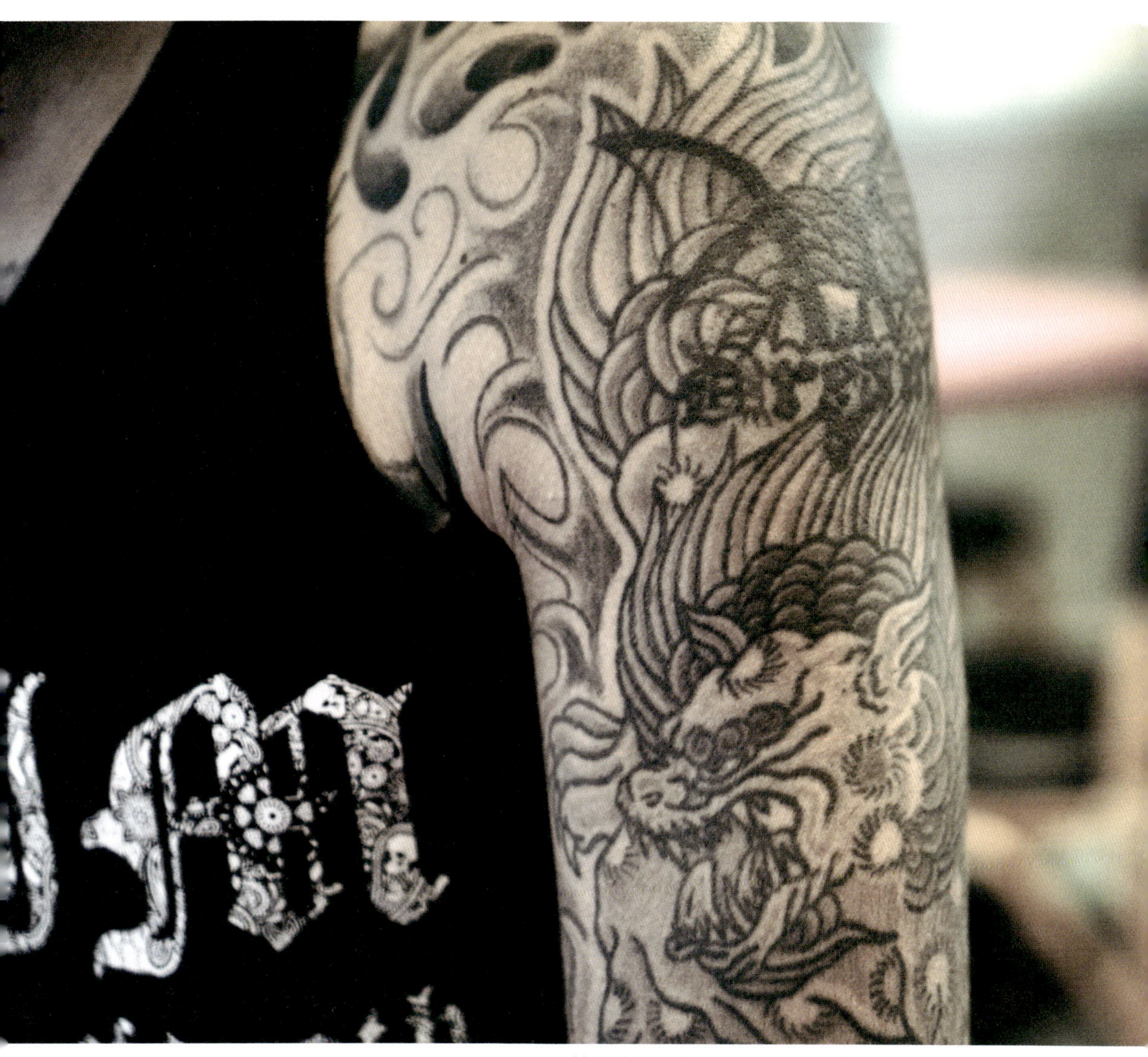

Komainu, a Japanese lion dog. Guardians against evil spirits.

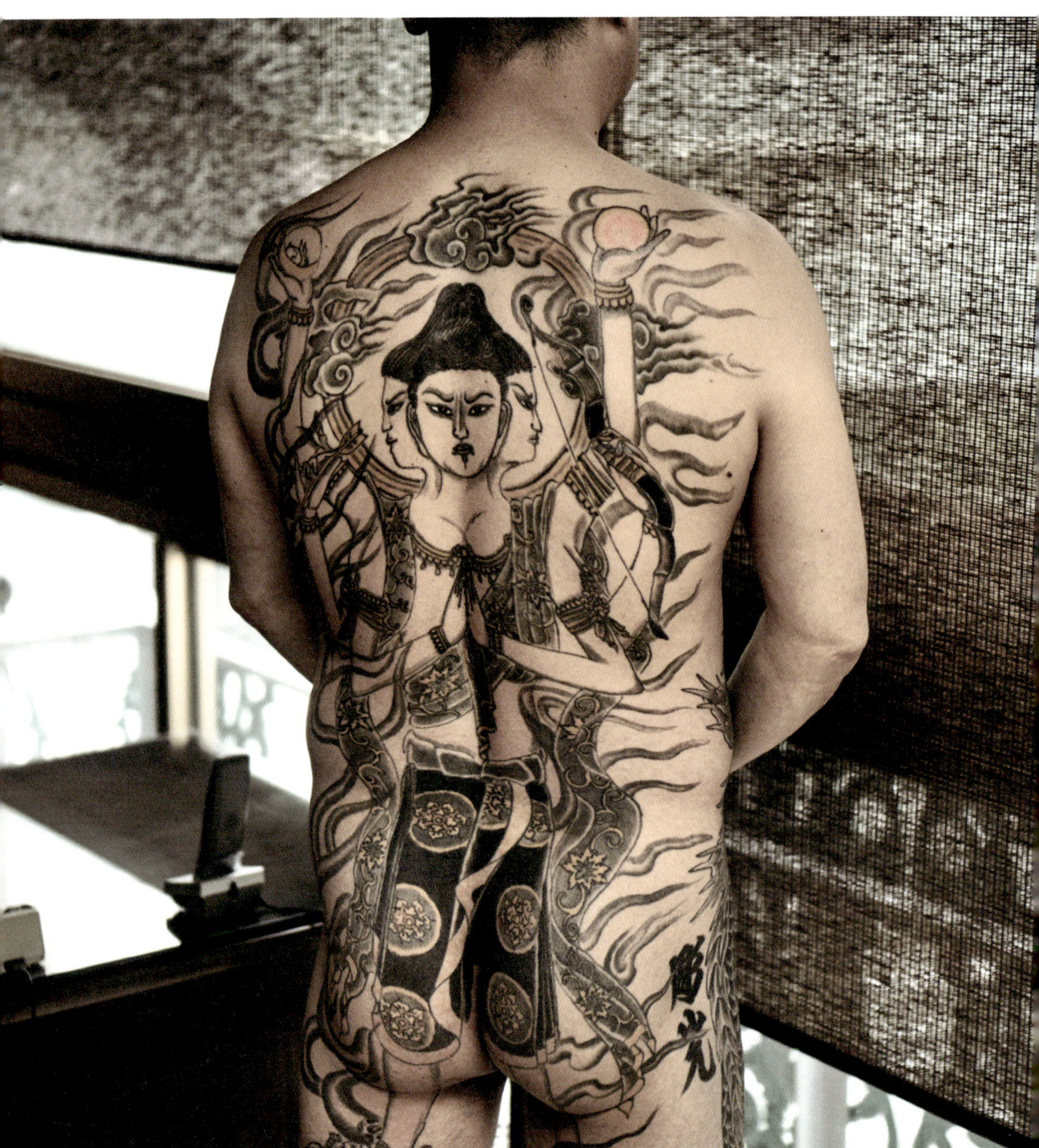

The irezumi on my back is really special to me. I have given it a lot of thought. I read about the history of the asura and I really liked it. It was perfect for me. In Japan, the asura have a bad story, but in India they have a different story. So it depends on how you read it and how you think about it.

Asura goddess holding the sun and the moon.

Modern Tattoos

Sometimes there is a shift in values between generations, and what used to be thought of as the norm no longer holds the same significance. Ever since *irezumi* began to be associated with the yakuza, they have been considered taboo by older generations in Japan.

For much of its history, Japan was a closed country, but after World War II it opened up, and due to the impact of globalization, the younger generation now has a different view of tattooing and tattoos. Not only has western culture influenced the younger generation and inspired the spread of western-style tattoos (not *irezumi)*, the global trend of getting tattoos in general has also led to the proliferation of traditional Japanese tattoos among ordinary citizens. These tattoos are sometimes called one-point tattoos, since they only cover one part of the body.

One of the yakuza who has traditional *irezumi* told me that, "I did the three dots on my hand out of curiosity when I was a kid, but there was no meaning behind it. I also did my zodiac sign on my wrist when I was younger." This development is frowned upon by the older yakuza generation. These tattoos are often referred to as "fashion tattoos", or it is said that they were made with a different intention or "a different heart."

Thanks to the global trend, it is not uncommon to come across tattoo studios that specialize in western-style tattoos in Japan today. Annual international tattoo conventions and the presence of tattoo magazines in the country have also contributed to the growing trend of westernized tattoos. It is interesting to see how this development has affected the yakuza tattoo culture. Since traditional *irezumi* take hundreds of hours to finish, some younger yakuza have discovered a short-cut for marking their bodies. Some of the yakuza that I met during my stay in Japan have traditional *irezumi* mixed with more modern designs. This is a method developed by a number of new tattoo artists. They mix old traditional motifs with new styles influenced by the West. Some of these tattoos resemble what one might expect to see in an American gangster movie, expressions of "thug life". Some younger yakuza only have modern-style tattoos, and there are also those who do not have any tattoos at all.

The boss, Ken-San, was very concerned when he heard I was writing about modern tattoos. He told me that, "these tattoos have nothing to do with traditional yakuza *irezumi* or culture." His concerns regarding modern tattoos reflect his opinions about the younger generation in general.

"I believe that many in the younger generation don't have the same heart as the older yakuza. Some young people get traditional *irezumi* just so they can look cool. Their hearts are not in the right place."

One young yakuza that I met is a perfect example of how the combination of modern and traditional tattoos is perceived. His stories suggest that he is divided between the social expectations that are connected to tattoos since he is a yakuza and he has more personal reasons for getting them. He explained his choice of motifs in a highly entertaining way. On his back, he had the traditional Japanese goddess Kanon, but he claimed that he only got it since "the god with many arms would be too painful." The boss, who looked at him with disappointment in his eyes, sighed deeply. The young yakuza continued by saying that he used to shoot crows and therefore felt compelled to get a tattoo of a crow on his arm, and how he once caught a bird with a fishing rod and therefore felt the need to get a tattoo depicting that too. He also had one of an anchor that represents his hometown, Yokohama. The last tattoo he showed me was a symbol that represents his belief in aliens, but before I got a chance to take a good photo of it, the boss, who had probably heard enough, said, "Let's go. I have a cut-off finger to show you."

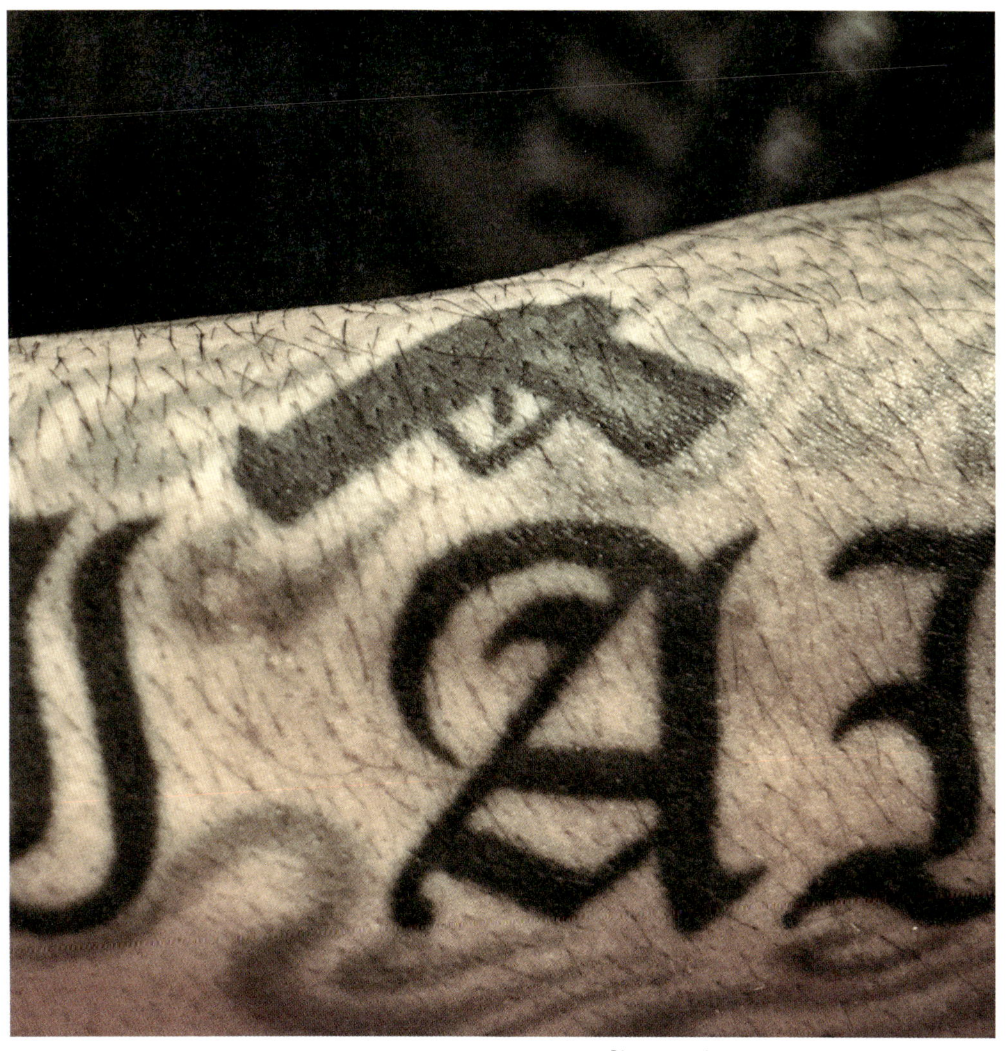

Close-up of a gun tattoo on a young yakuza.

My job was to take care of the gun. That's why I tattooed a picture of it. The big bosses don't carry guns, so I was the one protecting the gun, and I got the tattoo to commemorate that.

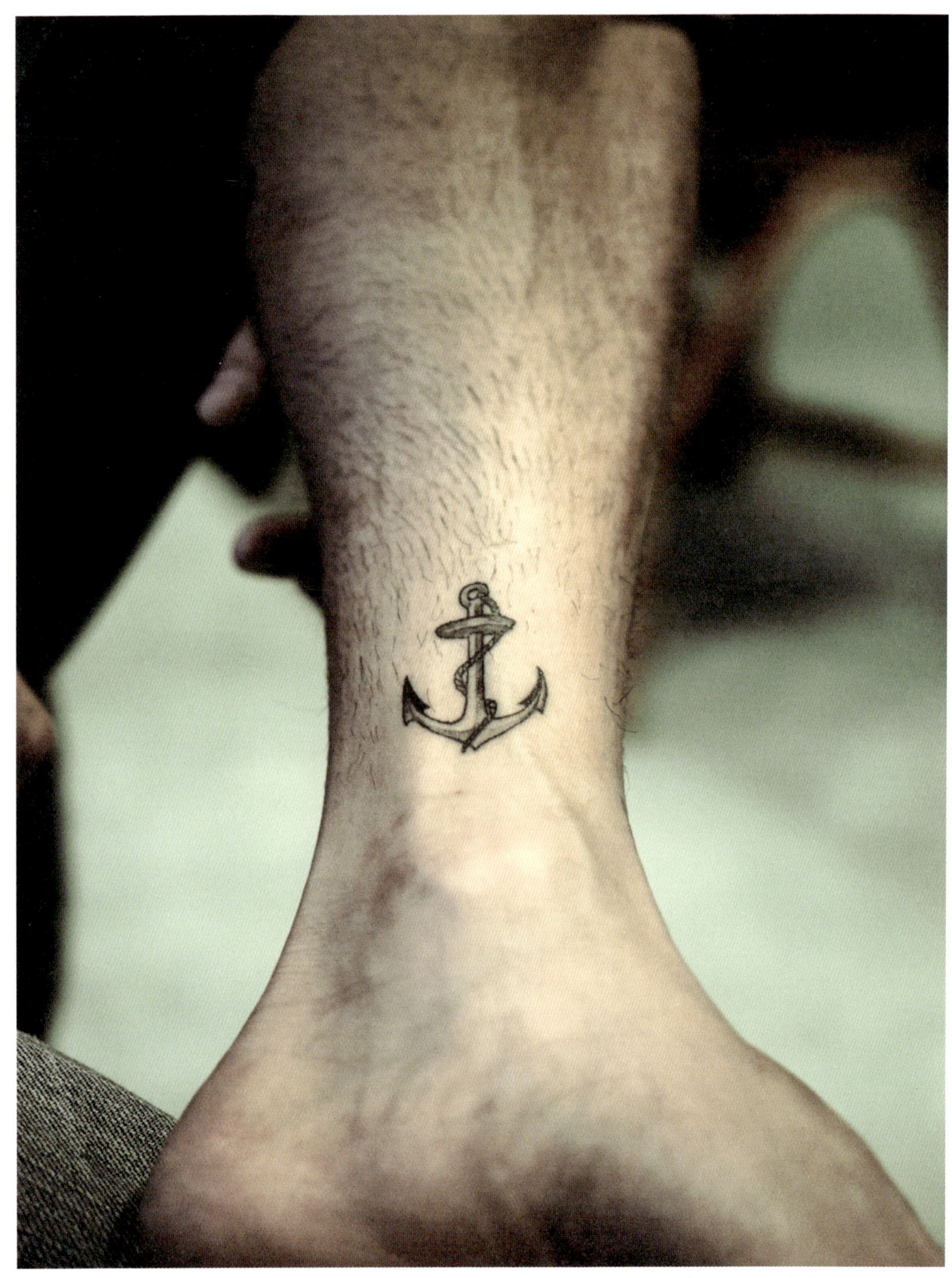

An anchor that symbolizes Yokohama.

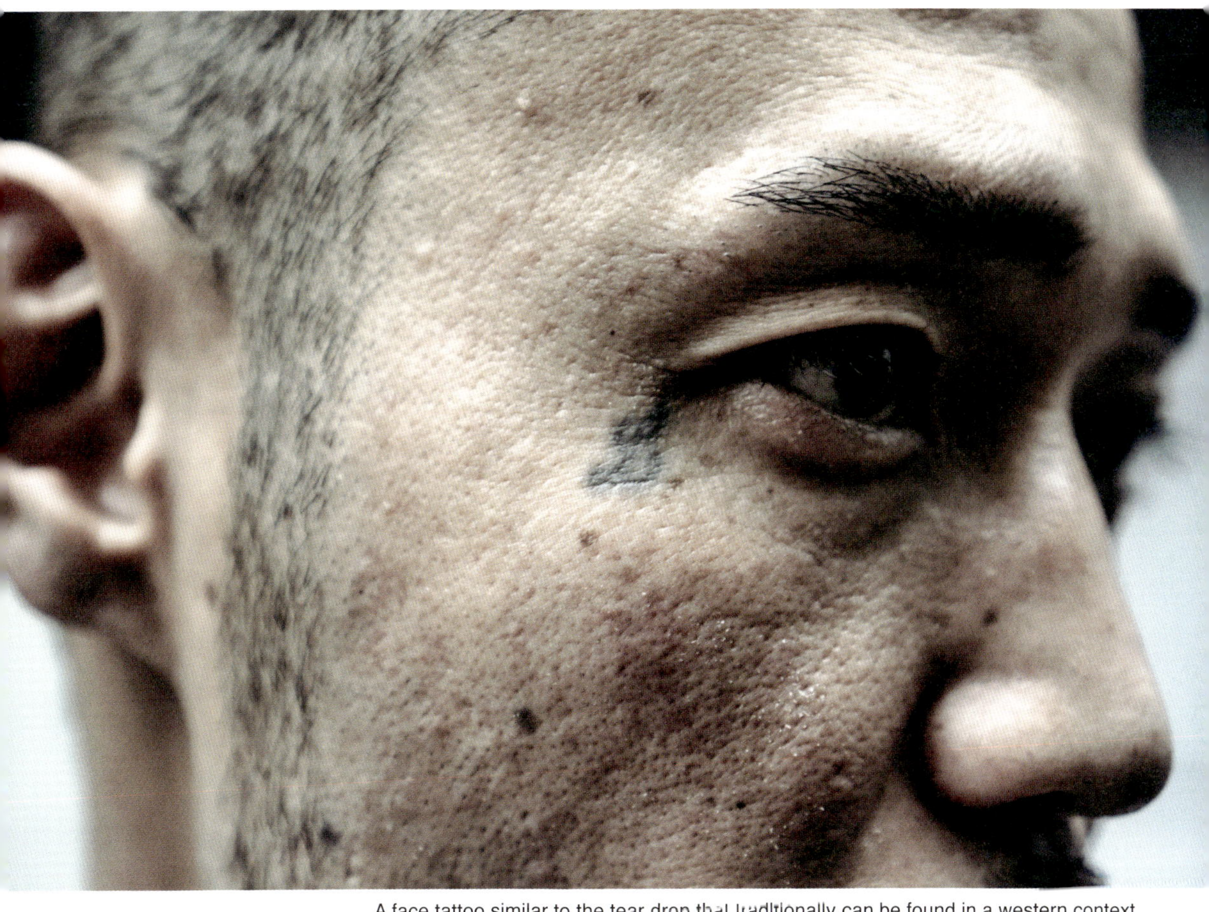

A face tattoo similar to the tear drop that traditionally can be found in a western context.

I got a tattoo on my face to remind me not to break the law. With a tattoo on your face, the police will recognize you and you can get busted. But I'll commit crimes either way. It's impossible for me to stick to the rules.

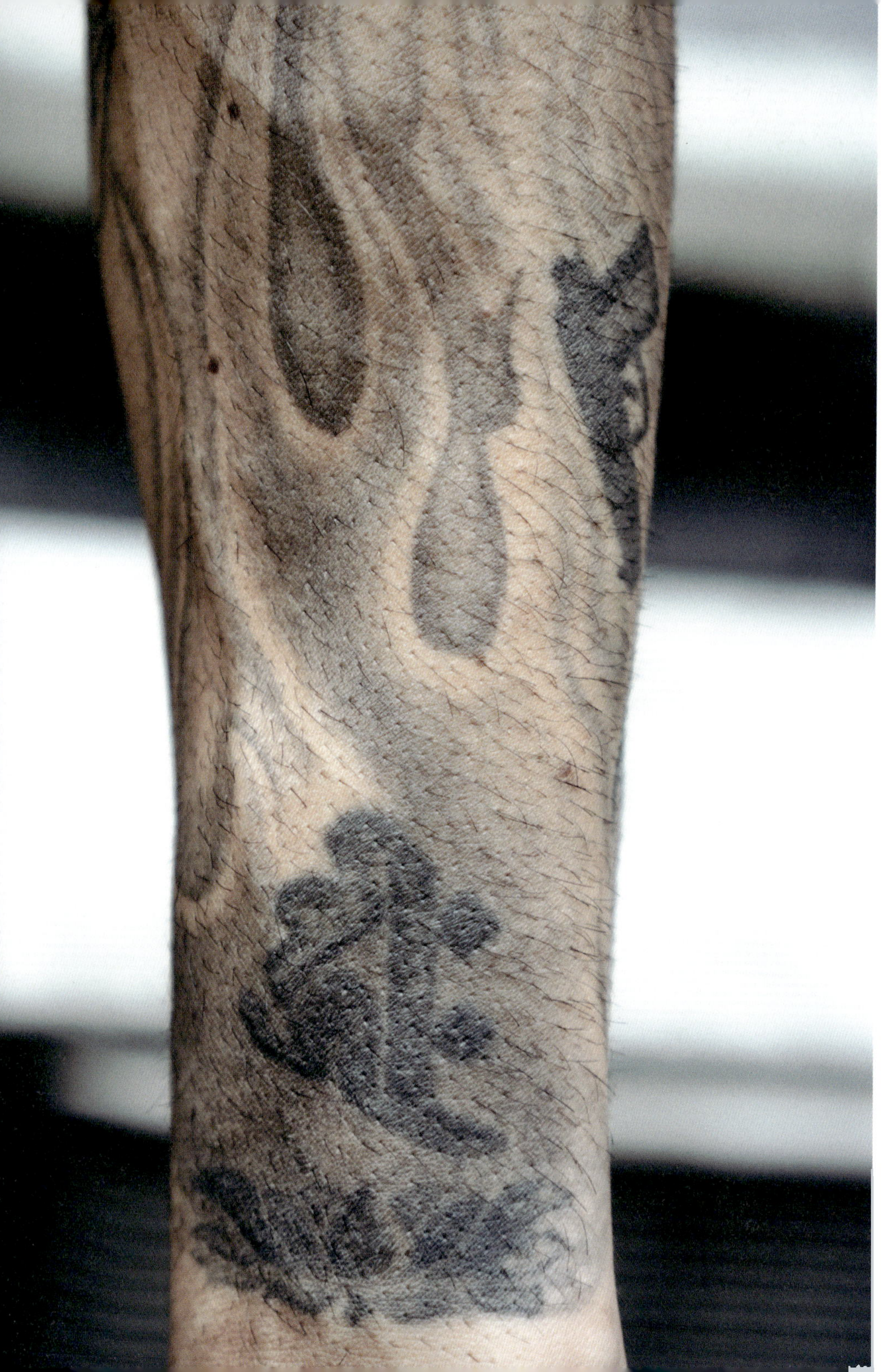

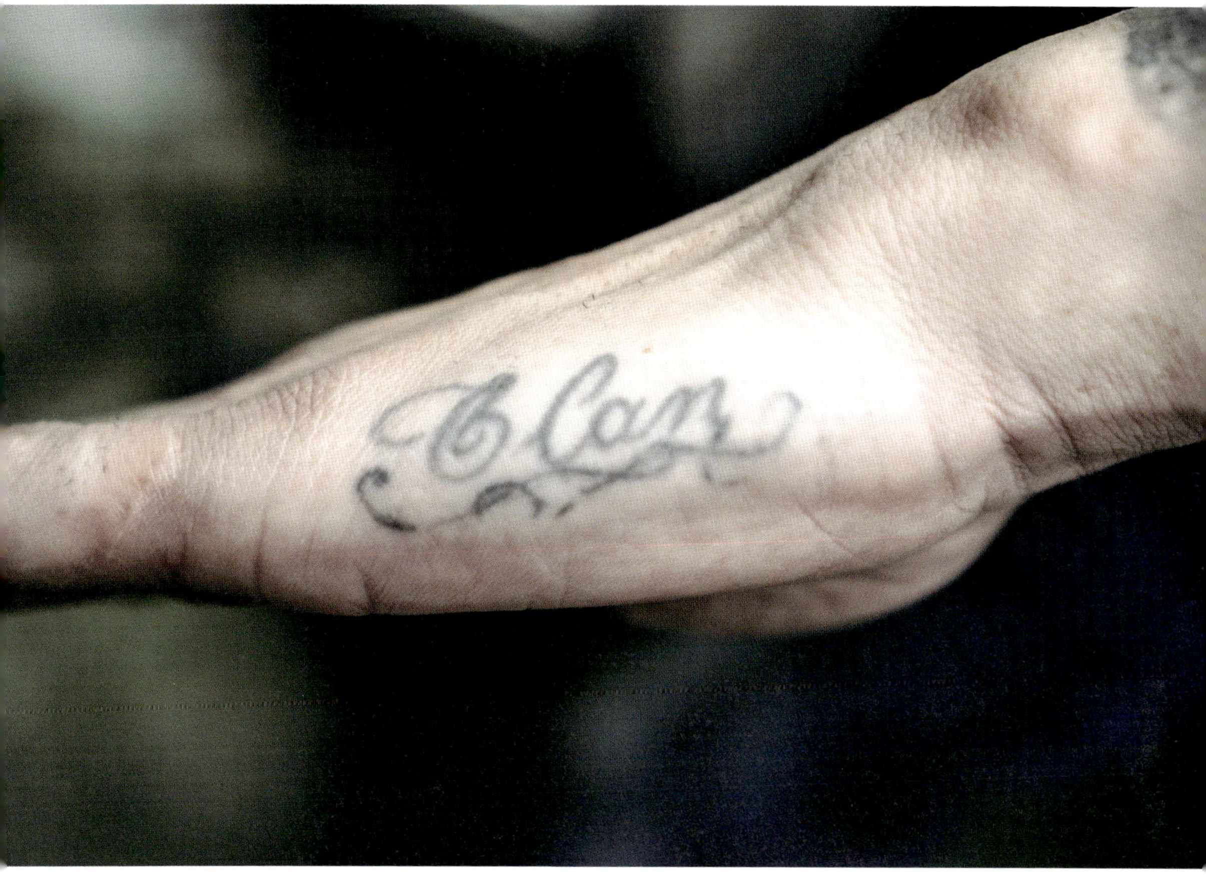

Latin script on a hand.

Flames tattoos, and an "A" in Latin script tattooed on an arm.

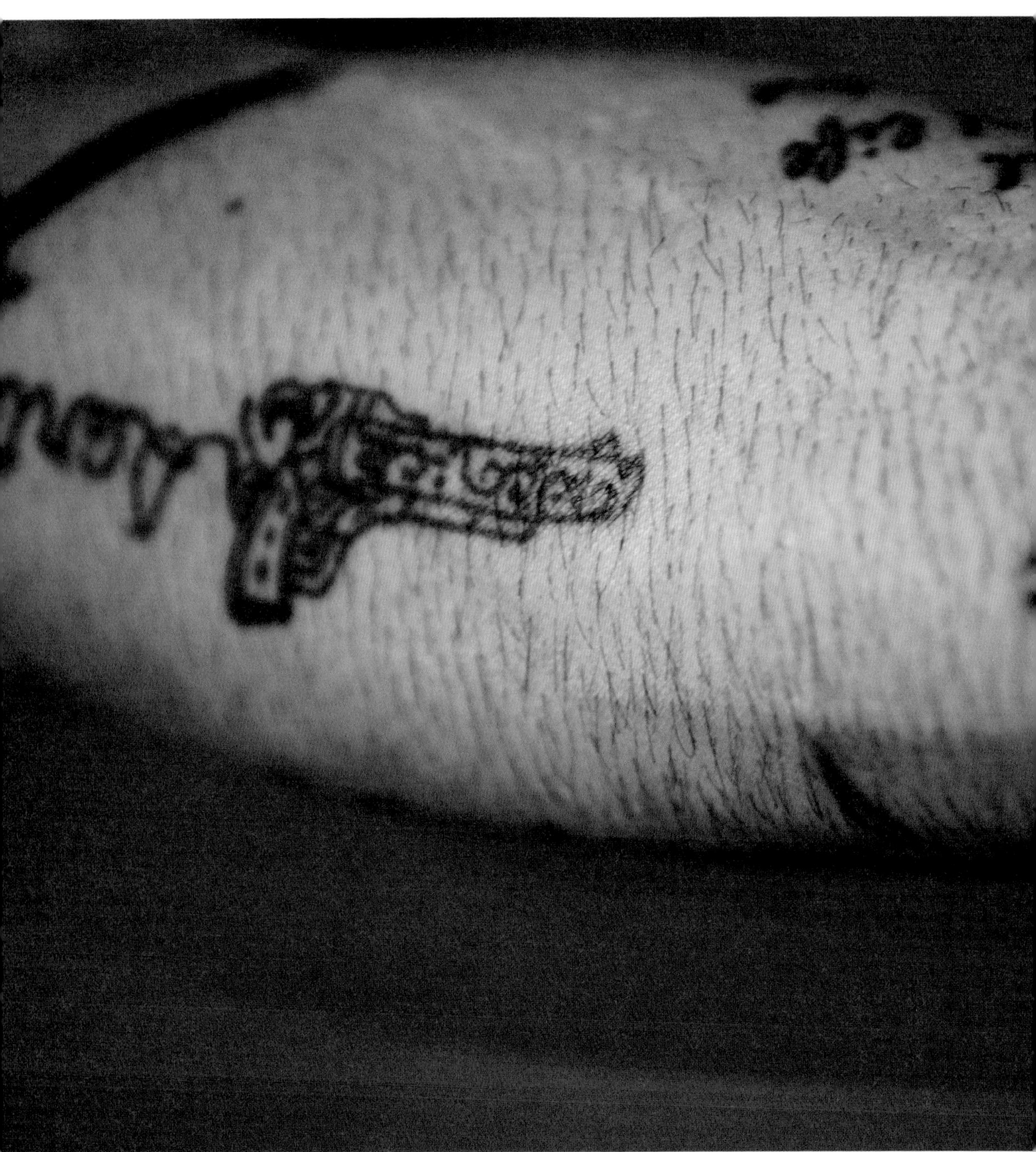

Close up of a tattoo of a gun.

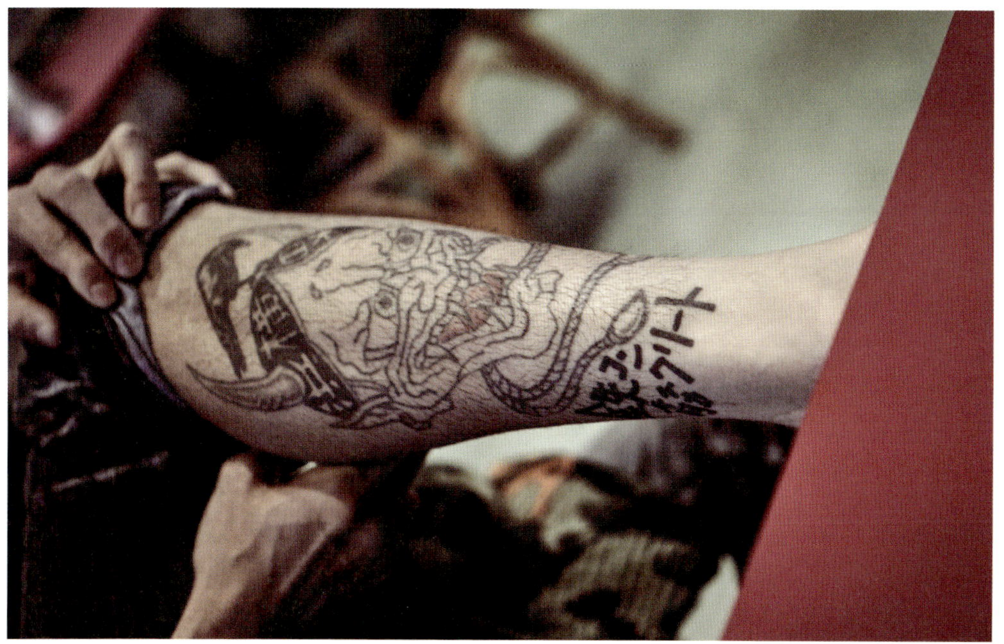

A traditional Hanya mask tattooed on a leg.

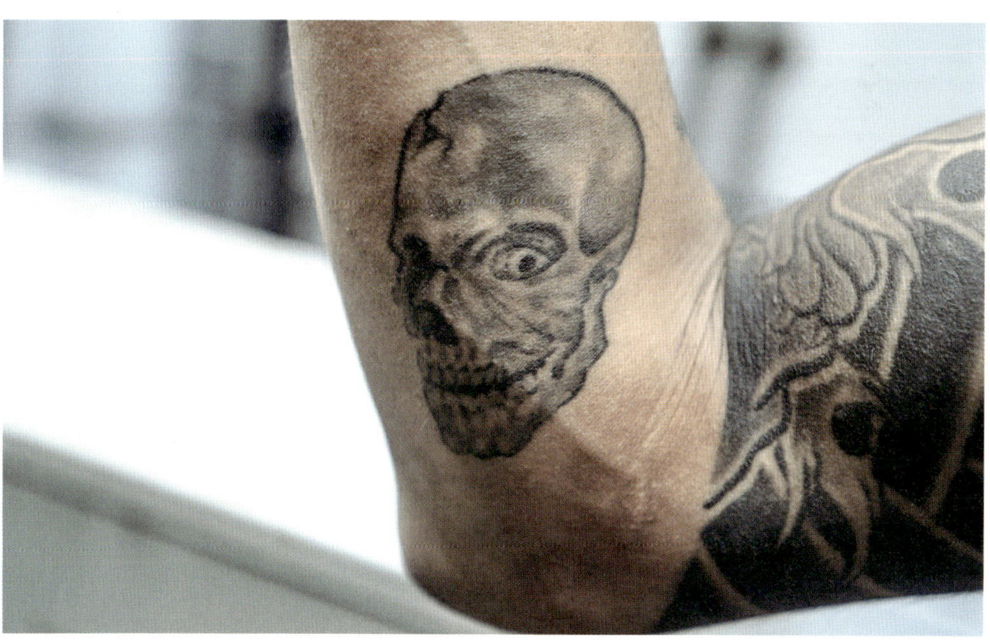

A modern skull tattoo on an arm.

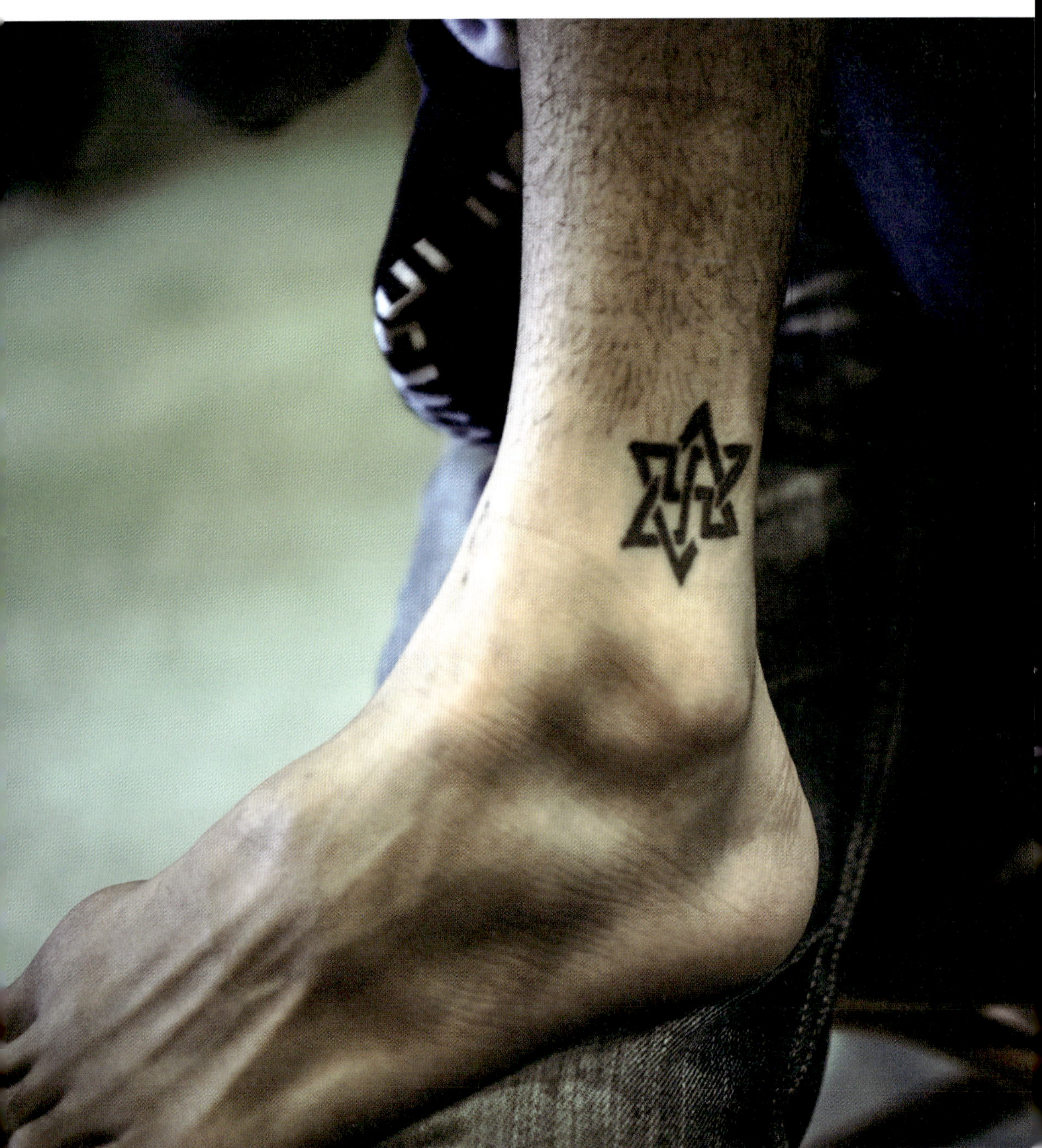

A personal symbol of belief in aliens.

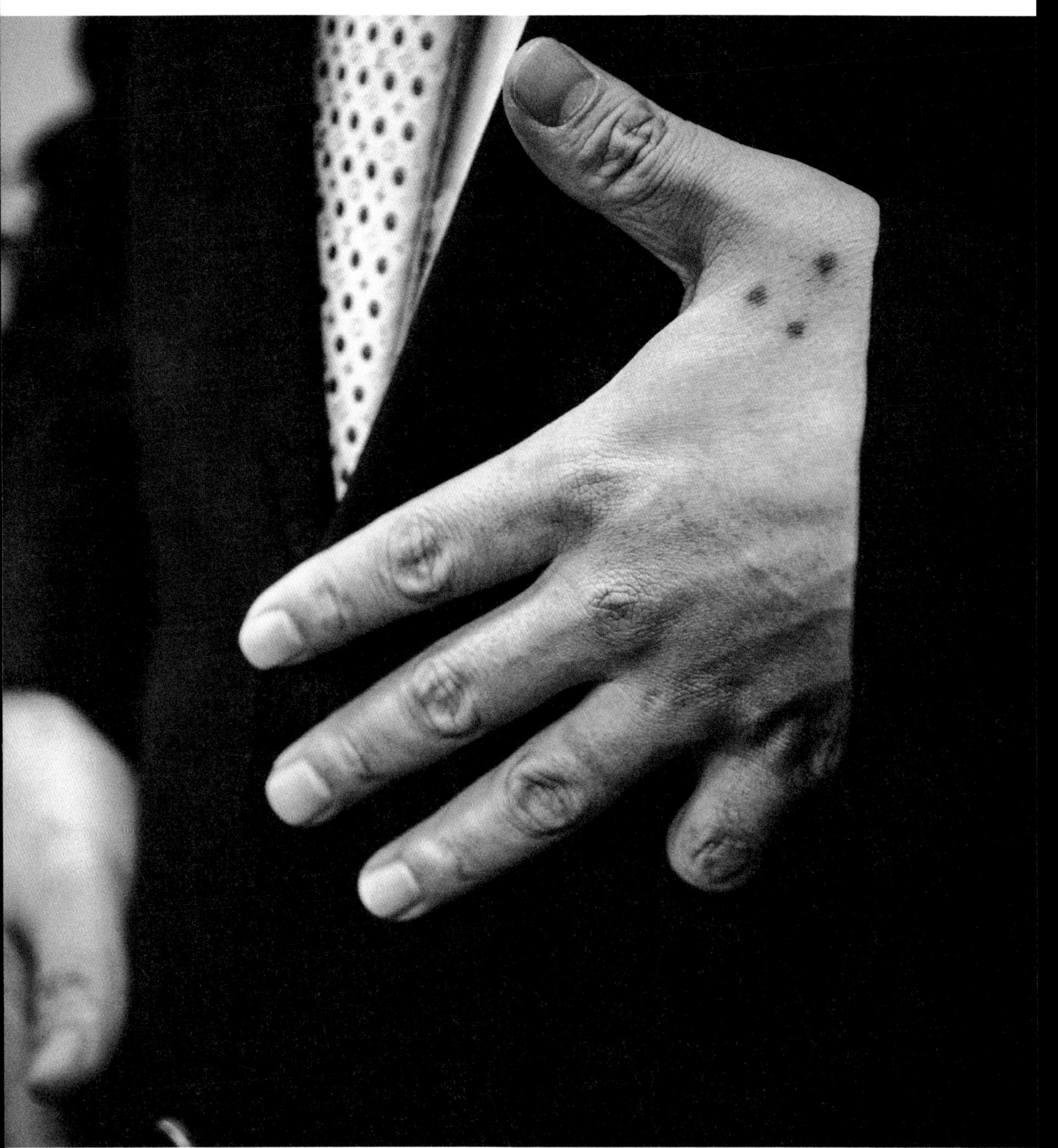

Three dots done in early life and a cut-off finger.

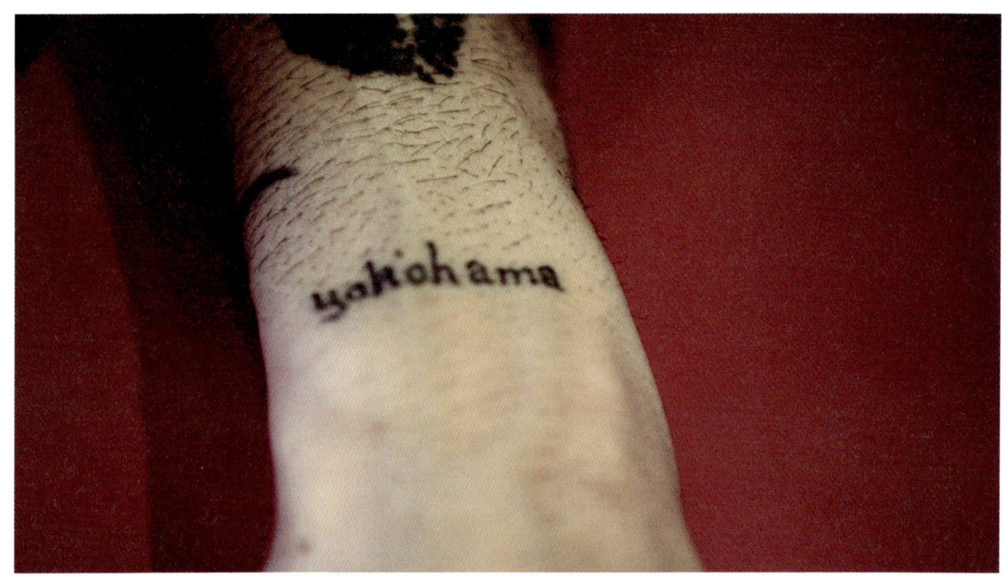

Yokohama in Latin script.

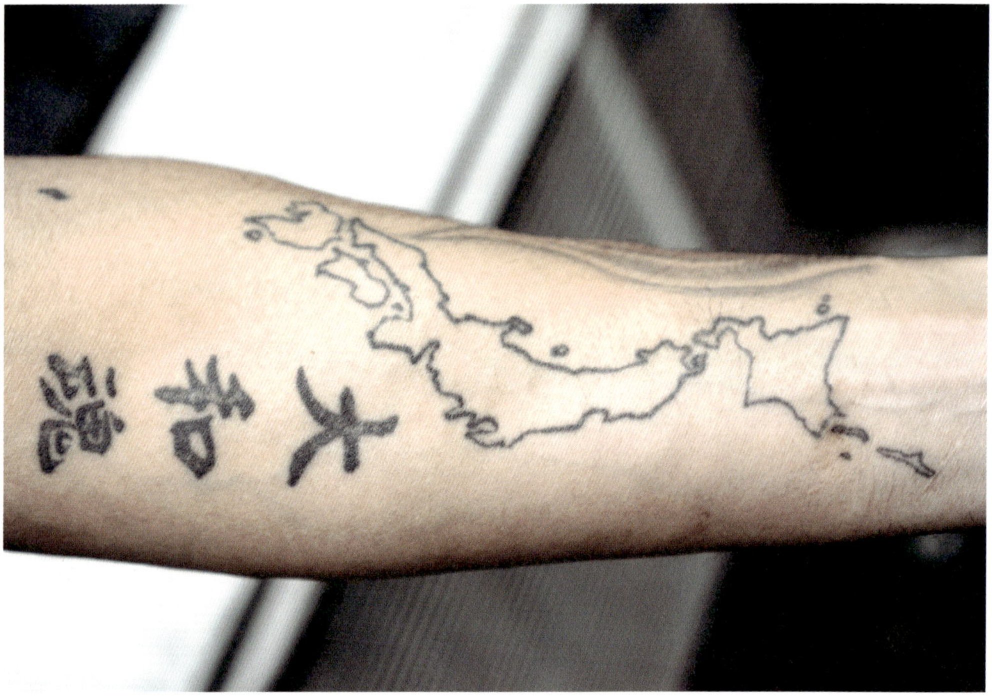

A map of Japan tattooed on an arm.

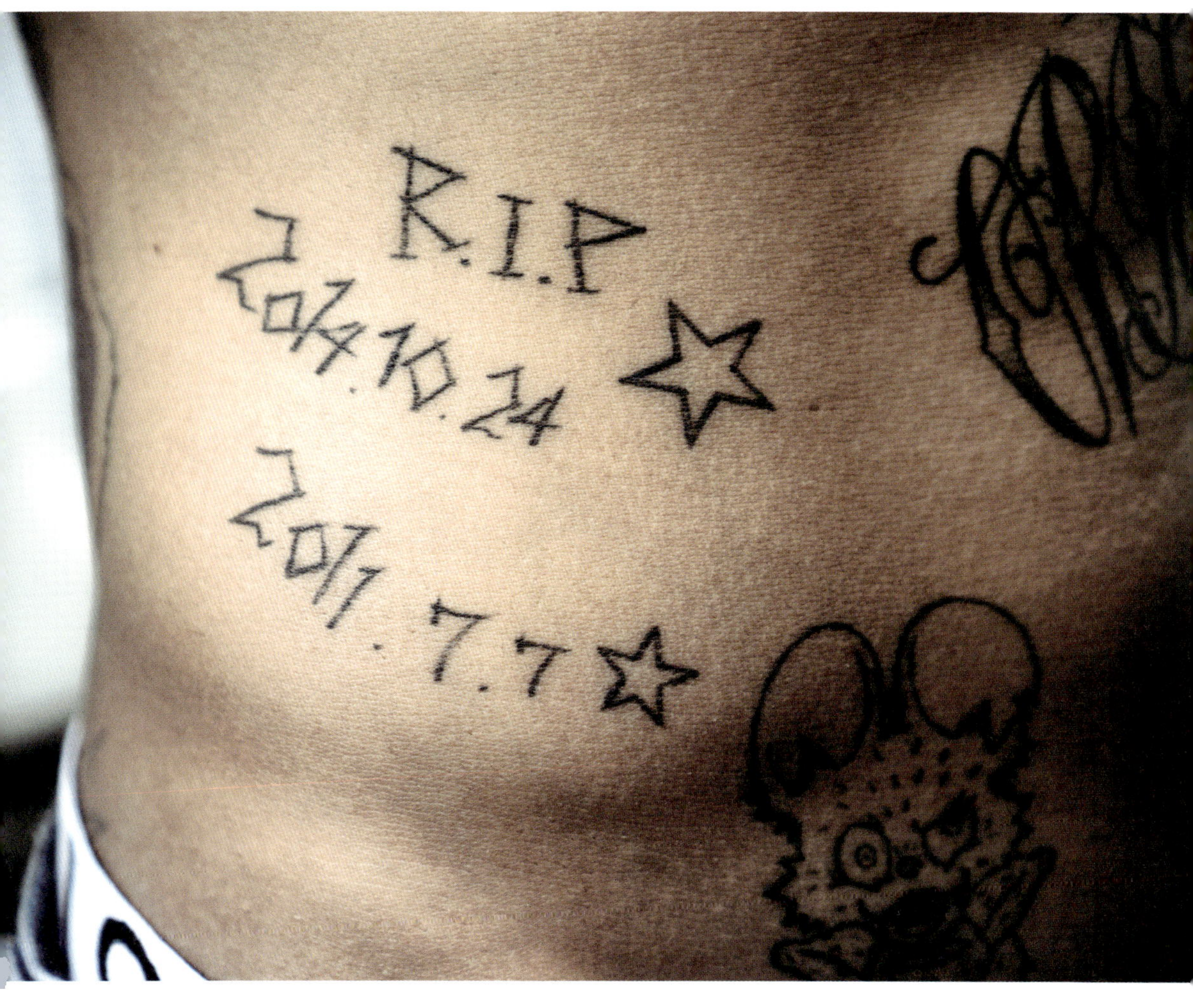

R.I.P. tattoo commemorating a yakuza's grandparents.

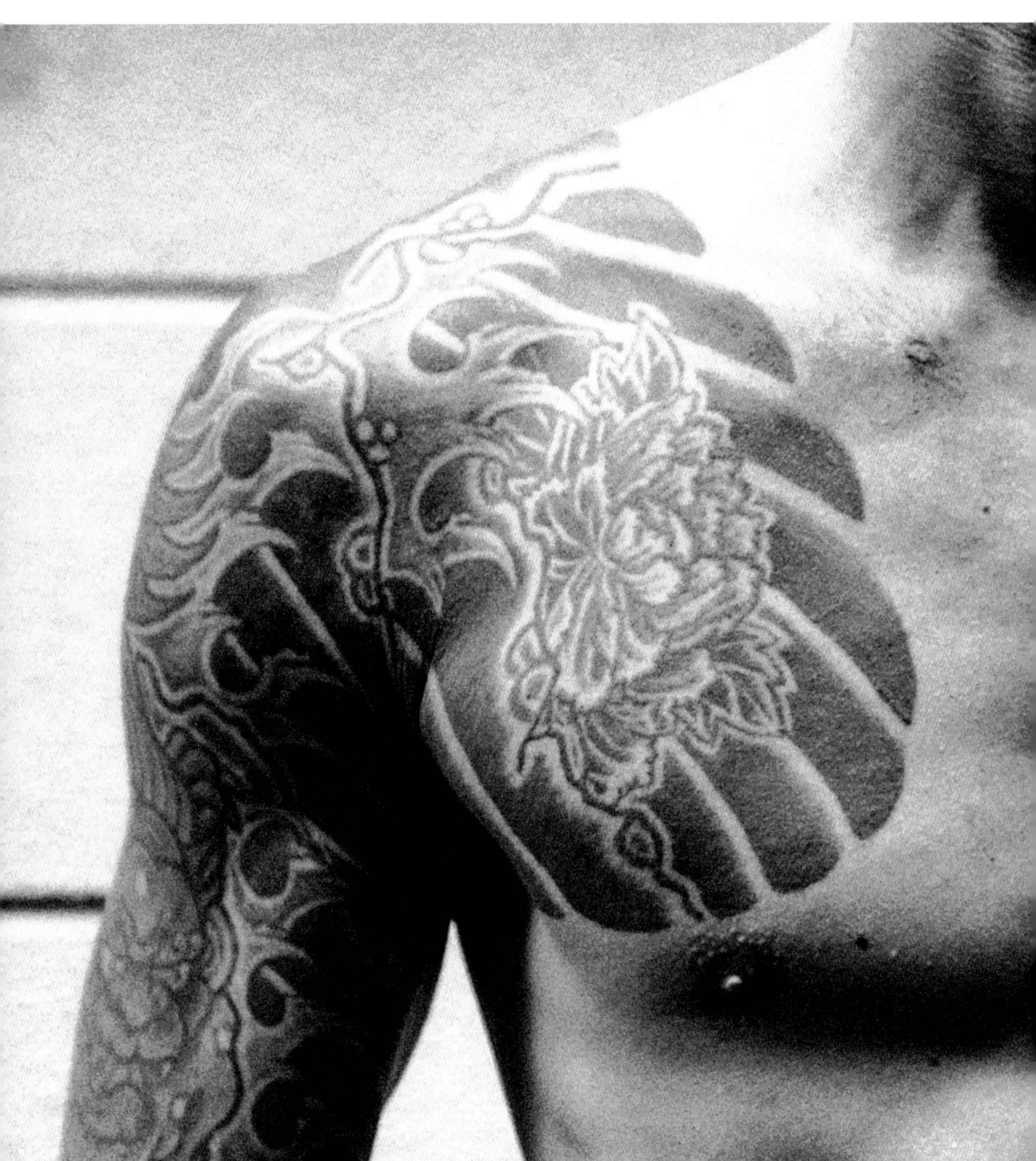

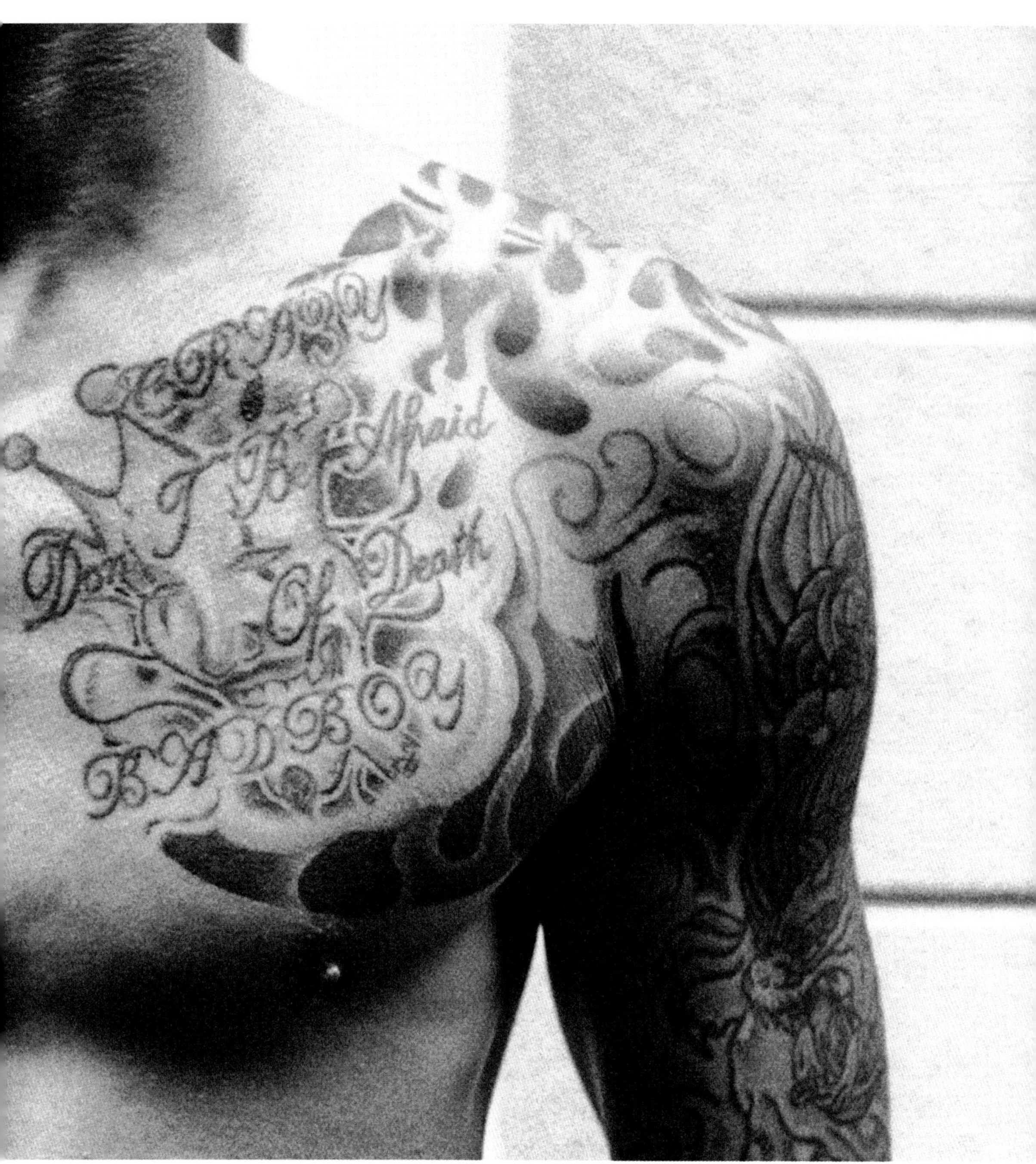

A mix of traditional *irezumi* motifs and new "westernized" motifs.

Second Family & Women

I am sitting in Ken-San's, the boss, kitchen when suddenly a door slams in the pleasant-looking apartment. The boss comes into the kitchen with a troubled look on his face and says, "That was the toughest negotiation ever." He had just convinced his 21-year-old daughter to let me photograph her tattoo.

Naturally, being a member of the yakuza is often combined with having a wife and children, another family alongside your yakuza family, and just like in any family, there will be ups and downs in the relationship between the family members. A yakuza boss is of course not immune to the will of a teenage daughter.

In some mafia-like organizations around the world, children will follow in their parents' footsteps and later join that organization. Even though there are examples of this happening within the yakuza, it is not common. Yakuza families, unlike some of their Italian counterparts, are not based on blood ties, but on the above-mentioned *oyabun–kobun* relationship. One member even told me that, "My child has never asked me about it, maybe she realizes that I'm a yakuza, but she never

asked." I found out from other yakuza that I interviewed that when choosing between their wives and kids, and the organization, the yakuza nearly always comes first. "If two things happen at the same time, you need to go to the boss instead of your wife, but if it's not really a problem, you can just go to your family. In your wife-family, you're the boss, but in the yakuza you have a boss. Yakuza comes first, then the family."

The yakuza environment is a masculine one. The role of the wife is subordinate and generally involves looking after the children. However, it does not mean that she does not have an ordinary job. Apart from the boss's daughter, the women I met during my stay with the yakuza were their friends or ex-girlfriends. I met them while I was hanging out with them in bars, clubs and so-called hostess bars. A hostess bar is a typically Japanese phenomenon. Here, you can have drinks and talk to women. They will flirt and talk with customers, pour their drinks and light their cigarettes, but they will not have sex with them.

Women who mix with yakuza do not necessarily know anything about the organization. Their social backgrounds, like those of the yakuza, are diverse. The wives and girlfriends of yakuza will occasionally get tattoos of their own.

If you ask a yakuza about the role of women in their organization, you will most likely be met with an answer similar to the one I was given, "There are no women in the yakuza." In general, this is probably true. According to the few reports that address this topic there are very few women yakuza, which is interesting because the yakuzas' European counterparts include women that have scaled the heights of their hierarchies. There are exeptions, however. Women have in some cases become temporary leaders, so-called *onna-oyabun*, or female godmothers, after the death of their husbands, but in general it seems that women are not active members of the yakuza, although some adopt the *irezumi* tradition.

Although the wife and children might not be present in the organization, they are visible on the members' tattoos, often by name.

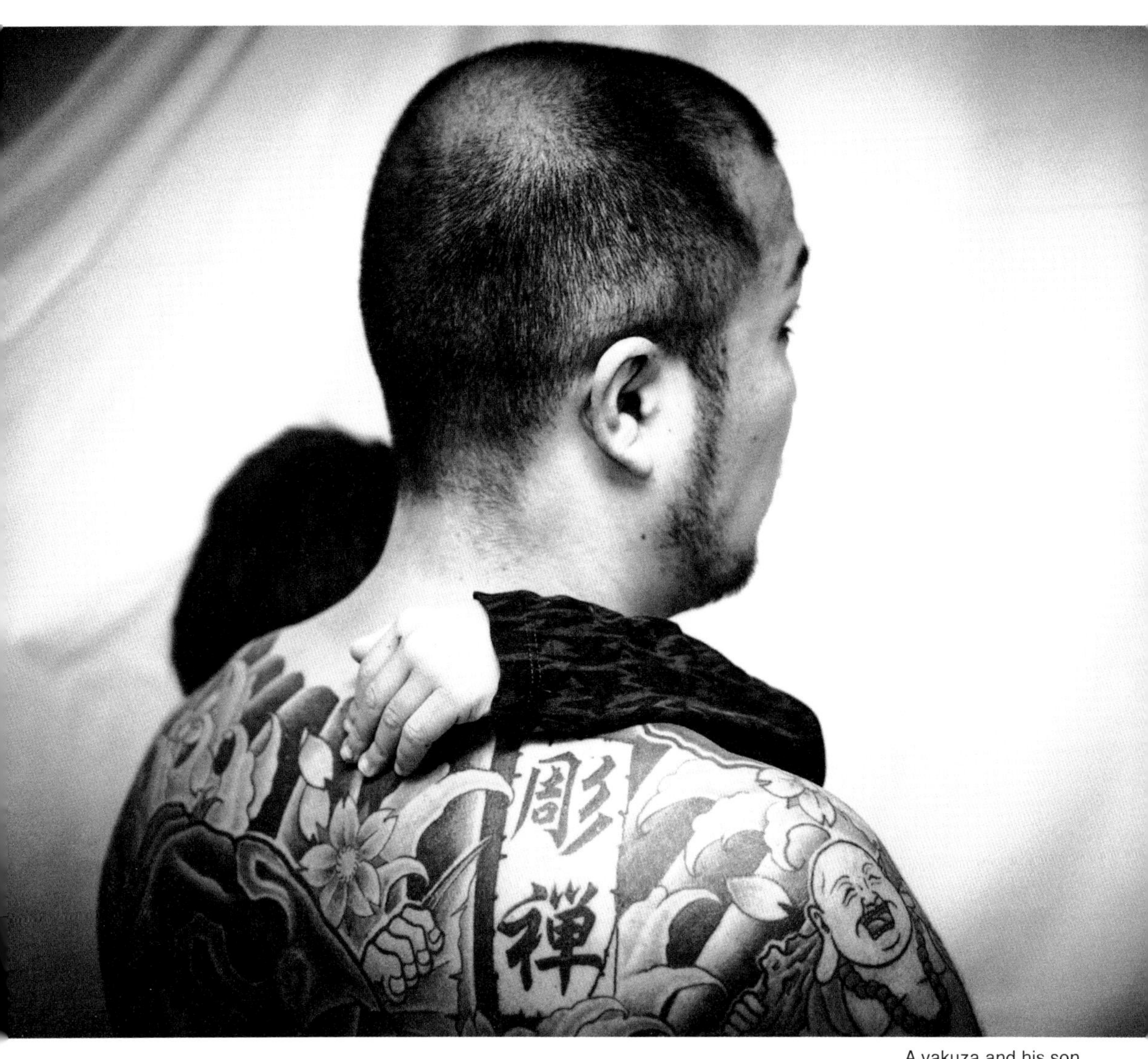

A yakuza and his son.

I love my son, but the boss always comes first.

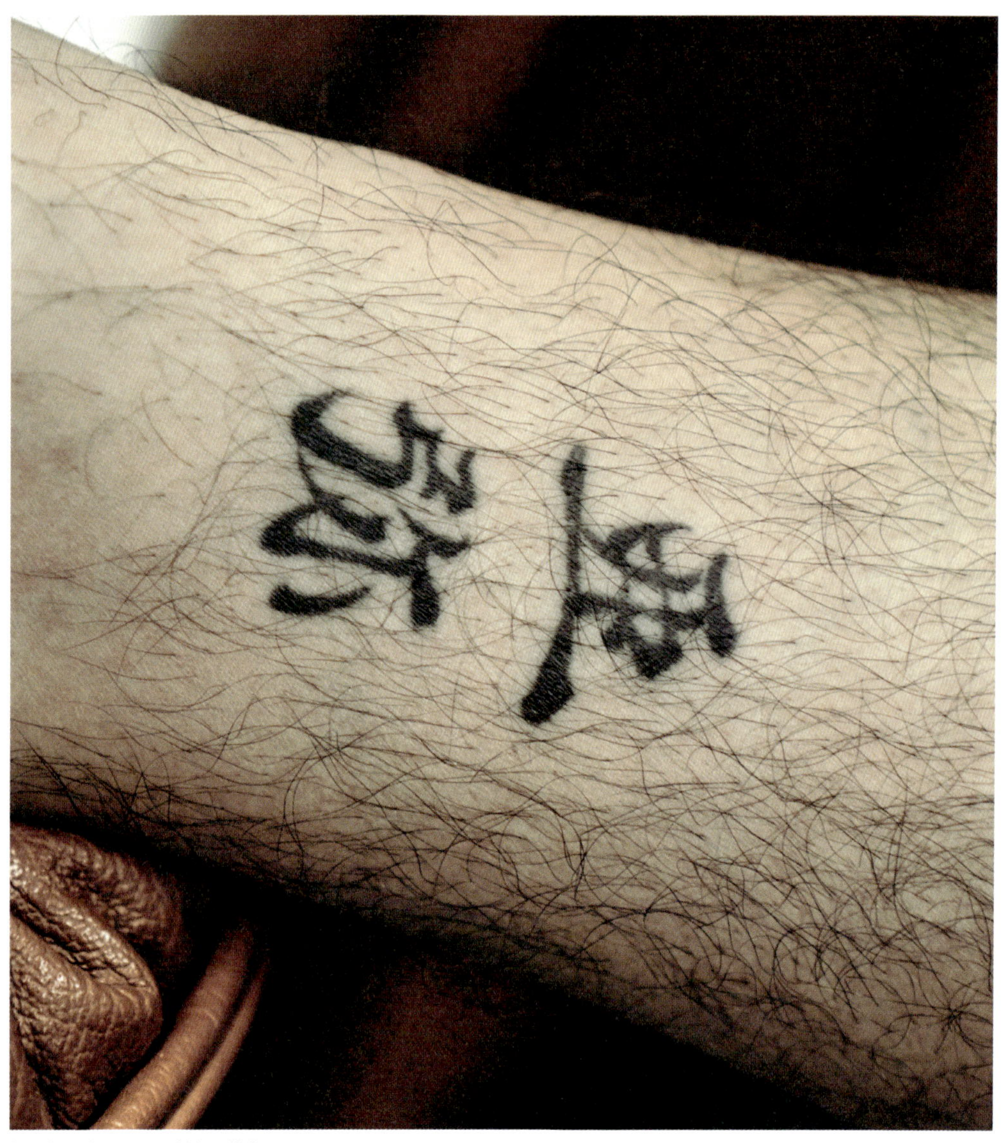

A yakuza's tattoo of his wife's name.

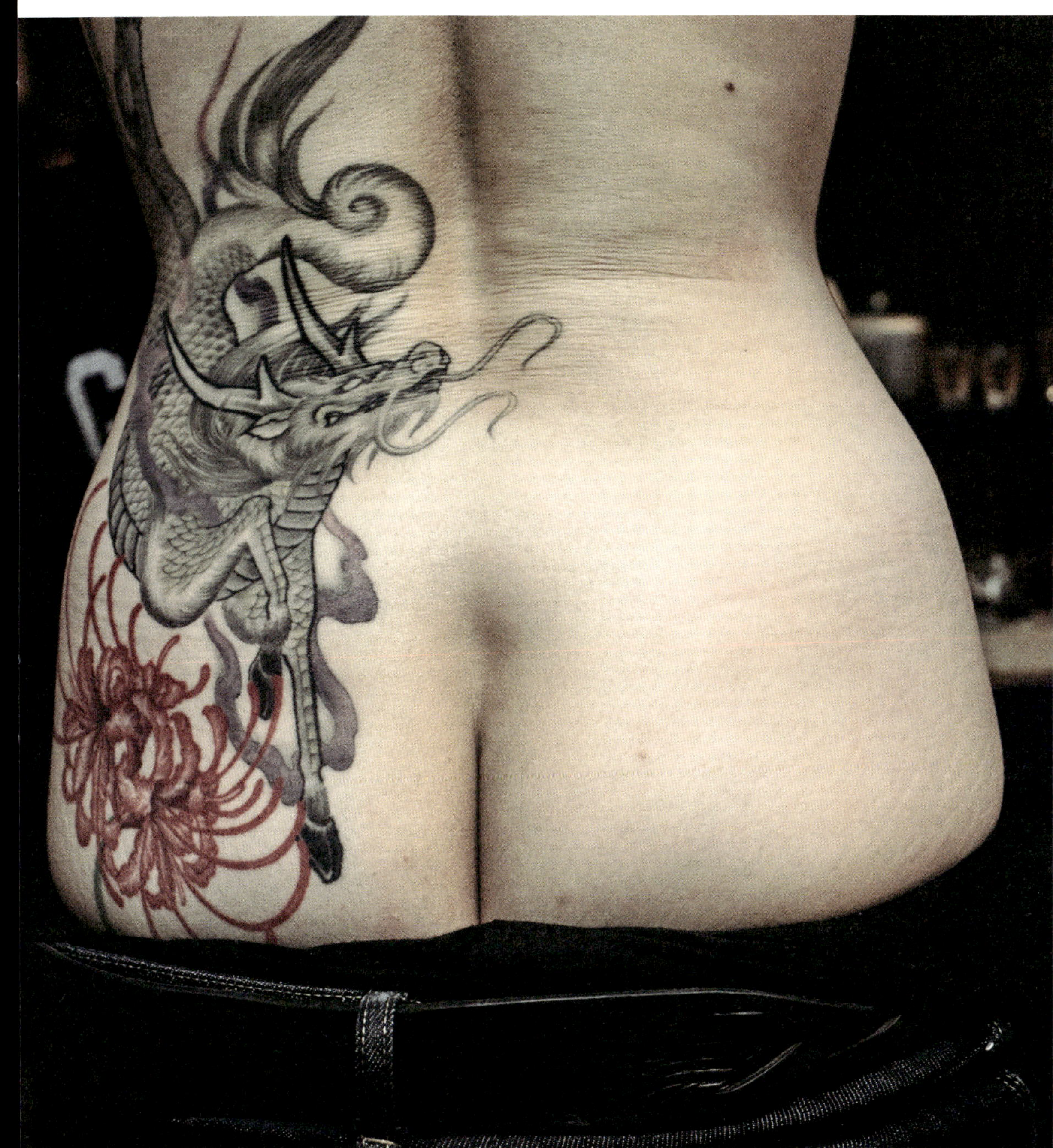

A yakuza's girlfriend's tattoo.

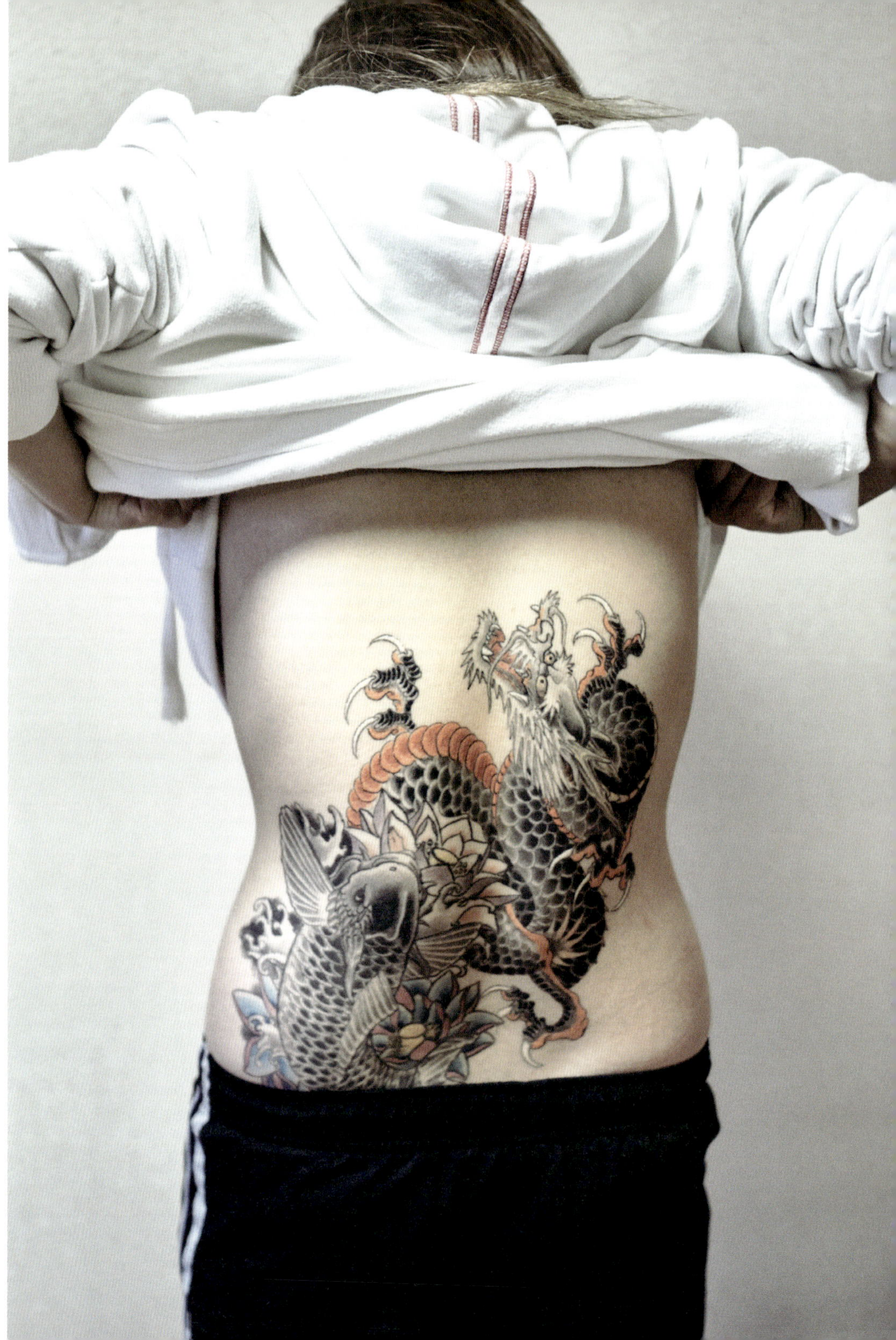

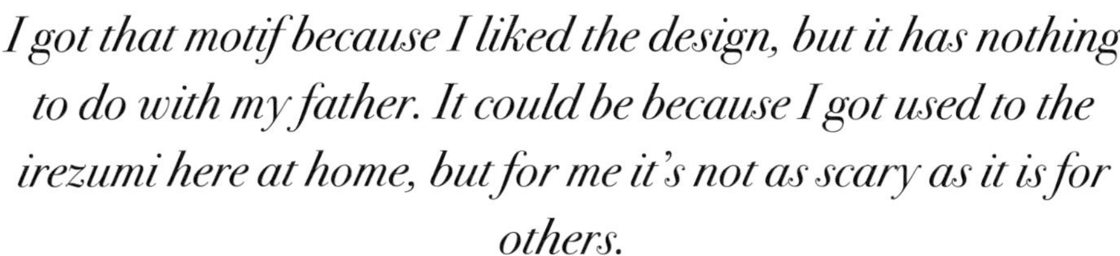

I got that motif because I liked the design, but it has nothing to do with my father. It could be because I got used to the irezumi here at home, but for me it's not as scary as it is for others.

A yakuza's daughter's *irezumi.*

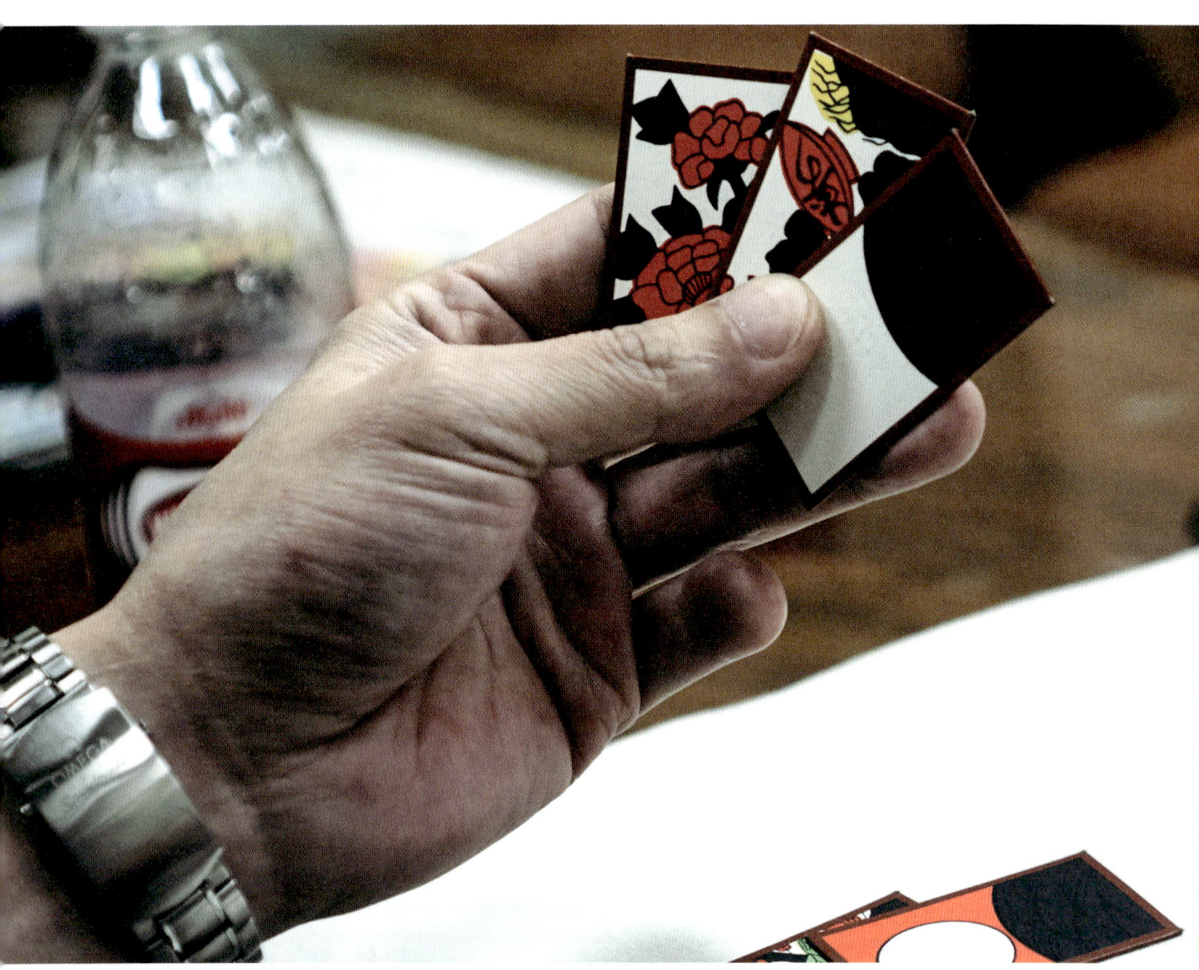

A yakuza playing with traditional *hanfuda* cards, displaying
his cut-off finger.

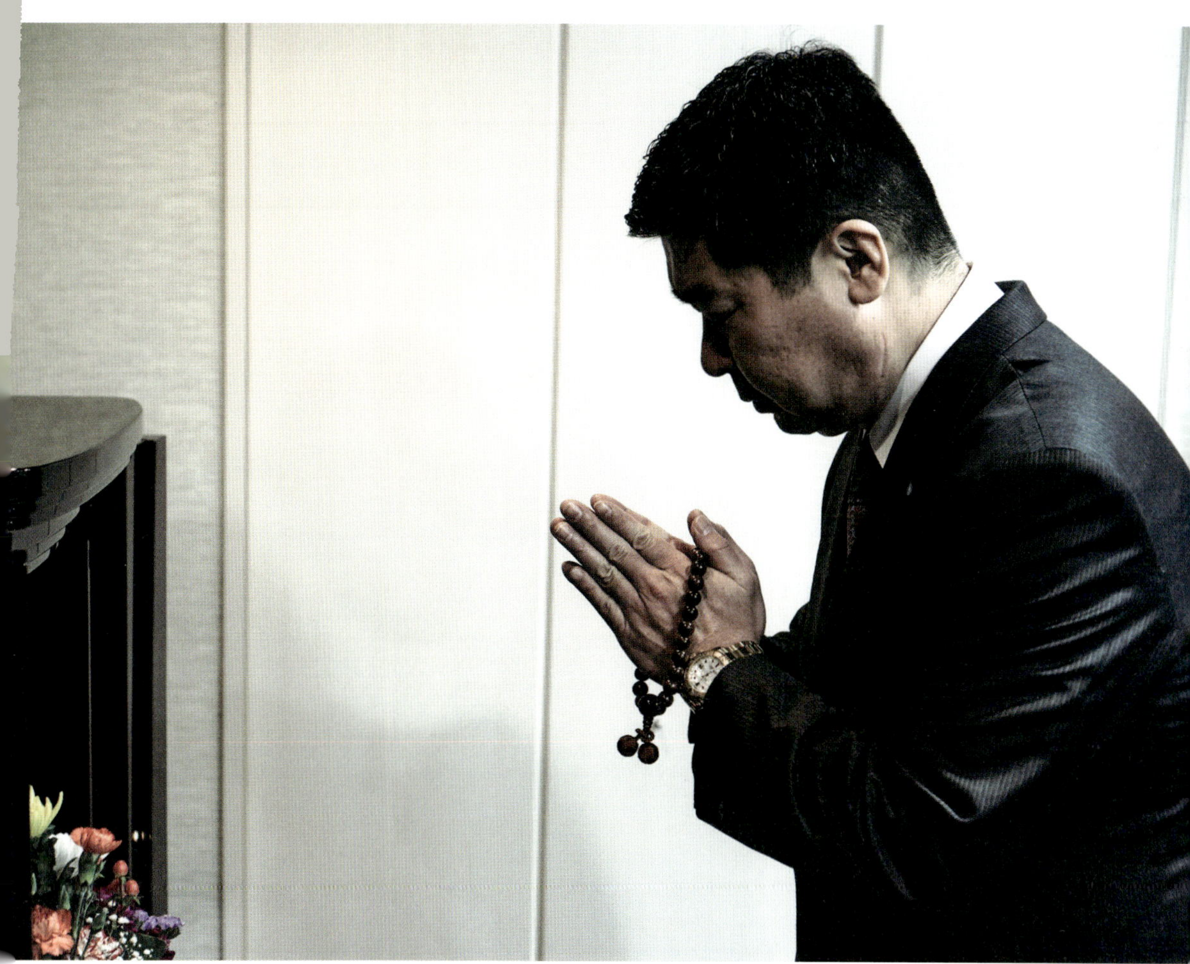

The boss praying at a butsudan shrine in the main office.

Andreas Johansson has a PhD in the History of Religions. He works at Lund University. He has a special interest in the religions of Asia and has conducted a number of field studies in South Asia, analyzing religious terminology and symbols used by non-religious organizations. Johansson is also an avid photographer.
www.andreasljoh.com

REFERENCES

Alkemade, Rié (2014). *Outsiders amongst ousideres: A cultural criminological prespective onn the sub-subcultural world of women in the yakuza underworld*. Oisterwijk: Wolf Legal Publisher.

Arvidsson, Stefan (2016). *Morgonrodnad : socialismens stil och mytologi 1871-1914*. Lund: Nordic Academic Press.

Collier, John JRr., and Malcolm Collier (1986). *Visual Anthropology – Photography as a Research Method*. New Mexico University Press.

Fellman, Sandi (1986). *The Japanese Tattoo*. New York: Abbeville Press.

Gilbert, Steve (2000). *Tattoo History: A Source Book*. New York: Juno Books.

Gragert, Lt. Bruce A. (1997). "Yakuza: The Warlords of Japanese Crime". In *Annual Survey of International & Comparative Law:* Vol 4: Iss: 1, Article 9.

Hill, Peter B. E. (2003). *The Japanese Mafia: Yakuza, Law, and the State*. Oxford: Oxford University Press.

Kaplan David E. and Alec Dubro (2003). *Yakuza: Japan's Criminal Underworld*. Berkeley, Los Angeles: University of California Press.

Kingston, Jeff (2011). *Contemporary Japan: History, Politics and Social Change since 1980s*. Oxford: Blackwell Publishing.

Lane, Richard (1978). *Images From the Floating World: The Japanese Print*. New Jersey: Chartwell Books INC.

McCabe, Michael (2005). *Japanese Tattooing Now: Memory and Transition*. Atglen: Shiffer Publishing.

Schreiber, Mark (2001). *The Darker Side; Infamous Japanese Crimes and Criminals*. Tokyo: Kodansha International.

Sedholm, Matti, et al. (2005). *Horiyoshi III – The art of the Japanese Tattoo*. Stockholm: Koala Press.

Thrasher, Fredric M. (1927). *The Gang*. Chicago: The University of Chicago Press.

Yamada, Mieko (2009). "Westernization and cultural resistance in tattooing practices in contemporary Japan". In *International journal of Cultural studies* Volume 12(4) 319–338. Sage Publication.